DADDY KING
An Autobiography

DADDY KING

An Autobiography

c . 1

The Rev.
Martin Luther King, Sr.,

with Clayton Riley

Foreword by Benjamin E. Mays

Introduction by Andrew J. Young

WILLIAM MORROW AND COMPANY, INC.

New York   1980

B
KING, M.L.

Library of Congress Cataloging in Publication Data

King, Martin Luther, 1899-
  Daddy King.

  Includes index.
  1. King, Martin Luther, 1899- 2. Baptists—
Clergy—Biography. 3. Clergy—Georgia—Atlanta—
Biography. 4. Atlanta—Biography. I. Riley,
Clayton, joint author. II. Title.
BX6449.K56A3   286'.133'0924 [B]   80-17411
ISBN 0-688-03699-6

Printed in the United States of America

First Edition

1 2 3 4 5 6 7 8 9 10

BOOK DESIGN BY MICHAEL MAUCERI

This book is dedicated to the memory of my wife, Alberta Christine Williams King; my sons, Martin Luther King, Jr., and Alfred Daniel Williams King; and my granddaughter, Esther Darlene King. It is also dedicated to my daughter, Christine King Farris; my grandchildren, Alveda King Beal, Yolanda Denise King, Alfred Daniel Williams King II, Derek Barber King, Martin Luther King III, Vernon Christopher King, Dexter Scott King, Isaac Newton Farris, Jr., Bernice Albertine King, Angela Christine Farris; and my great-grandchildren, Jarrett Reynard Ellis, Eddie Clifford Beal III, and Darlene Ruth Celeste Beal.

From the days of our courtship until her tragic death on June 30, 1974, my wife was the quiet courage by my side in all of my endeavors. My sons, whose works have spoken for themselves, moved with courage to do what they knew was right. My daughter, Christine, has worked with the legacy of her mother's quiet courage and her own strengths to make her statement in the tradition of the values which we instilled in her.

My grandchildren, who range from a Georgia State Representative to a high school junior, have brought me untold hours of joy and happiness in their quests for the meaning of their own lives. They are the New South for which I have worked since the days of my youth.

Finally, this book is dedicated to my great-grandchildren, on whom the mantle will fall to continue the legacy of their ancestors.

Foreword

Martin Luther King, Sr., was born free, free as the wind that blows, free as the birds that fly. Let me prove this assertion:

At Stockbridge, Georgia, at the time, a Negro was not born human but was born a Negro—and "a Negro" meant that you were inferior and had no rights that the white man had to respect. "Daddy King," as he is affectionately called, was born in Stockbridge, a few miles from Atlanta, in 1899. At fourteen, Daddy King left Stockbridge and went to Atlanta and got a job as a fireman on the railroad. The train went through Stockbridge, and he told his mother that when he went through the town he would blow the whistle. His mother did not want her son to be on the railroad, so she visited the Southern Railroad officials and told them that her son had put his age up and that he was not of age to be working. They let Daddy King go.

In those days, a dishonest landowner—and there were many—cheated his tenants. In renting land, the first bales of cotton ginned, whether two, three, or four bales, went to the owner, but the cottonseed money went to the renter. Young King's father was cheated. The boy heard the owner tell his father that he had broken even and was out of debt. Young King said to his father,

"Ask him about the cottonseed money, Daddy!" The boss, incensed over this young black participating in his father's business, told young King to shut up. King's father told Martin Luther to keep quiet and go away. King's father had kept an account of what he spent and he was comparing his figures with the owner's figures. The white owner insisted that his figures were right. Young King hollered out, "Daddy, ask him about the cottonseed money!" This was a courageous thing for a young black boy to do in Stockbridge around the close of the nineteenth century.

Another incident is worth noting. One day King's mother sent him on an errand in Stockbridge. A white man interfered with the errand. He wanted young Martin Luther King to do something else, but the boy refused. In those days, a Negro was to do what a white man told him to do. For this refusal, the man beat Martin Luther. When Martin Luther got home, he told his mother what the white man did to him, and she went to the white man and beat him up. If this isn't a sign of freedom in the parents of Daddy King, I don't know what freedom is. This is from King's side of the family.

The Reverend A. D. Williams, father of Alberta Williams King, displayed equal bravery. He was the first President of the National Association for the Advancement of Colored People (NAACP), shortly after the NAACP was organized in 1910. The NAACP was a dangerous organization so far as the South was concerned, for it was fighting for the civil rights of black people. This was dangerous not only in Rev. Williams' time but was dangerous in 1954 when the NAACP won its case in *Brown* v. *The Board of Education* before the United States Supreme Court.

It isn't surprising that Martin Luther King, Jr., the son of Martin Luther King, Sr., became the greatest civil rights leader in this century. Like his father, Martin Luther King, Jr., was born free, free as the wind that blows and free as the birds that fly.

—BENJAMIN E. MAYS, President Emeritus, Morehouse College; President, Atlanta Board of Education

Acknowledgments

Through the grace of God, I have been granted a full, rewarding, and long life. Not in my most extravagant dreams, as I walked behind the plow or curried the mules in Stockbridge, Georgia, where I was born and spent the first nineteen years of my life, did I ever envision myself having the vast body of experience which I have had during my lifetime.

The South of my boyhood and most of my early life created conditions in which many black people and white people were fatally crushed. Why the God who led Moses and the children of Israel through the Red Sea, and David against Goliath, enfolded me in His care these eighty-odd years, I cannot answer, but I do know:

I love the Lord,
He heard my cry, and pitied every groan;
As long as troubles shall arise, I'll hasten to His throne.

My life has been chronicled for history because I hope and pray that it will be an inspiration to the young people who read it not to be overwhelmed by the odds against them, and I offer my fervent prayers that succeeding generations will not have to struggle to prove to themselves and to this great nation of ours their human worth, as I have had to struggle to prove mine.

I have been enormously supported by persons known and unknown, from around the world, during the tragic times which I have faced. I am indebted to each one of them. I have also been greatly supported and encircled in love during the moments of unspeakable joy which have come to my life. It would be impossible to reveal the names of everyone who has encouraged me and enabled me to bring this work to its completion. However, I am compelled to mention the persons whose names follow.

Miss Lillian D. Watkins, who for more than thirty years served as my secretary and financial secretary for Ebenezer. Miss Watkins is a dedicated churchwoman, and a friend to our family for whom the hour was never too dark if we needed her. Though now retired from Ebenezer, Miss Watkins continues to work with me, as do Mrs. Sarah Reed and Mrs. Bernice Thompson, the current secretaries at Ebenezer, who willingly give their assistance whenever it is required. Mrs. Melinda K. O'Neal shares her secretarial and clerical skills on a part-time basis with me.

Mr. Felton Sims, though carrying a full schedule as the custodian of Ebenezer, is never to busy to "run" me wherever I need to go, or run interference through the crowds that occasionally catch me in the office at the church.

Mrs. Esther Smith, a multi-talented lady whose limitless dedication to Ebenezer and love for our family has made her an invaluable ally for more than thirty years. Her unruffled disposition and thorough knowledge of the Baptist Church made her a key figure in the transition from my pastorate to that of the Reverend Joseph L. Roberts, Jr.

My grandchildren and my grandson-in-law, Dr. Eddie Clifford Beal, have been immense sources of comfort to me as they have graciously consented to perform small chores at my home and to serve as drivers and traveling companions.

Mrs. Rosa Sturgis, her daughter Deborah, and the Reverend Fred C. Bennette have assisted me in many ways.

Since the passing of my wife, I have learned to count very heavily on Mrs. Watha Walker, who was our housekeeper before Bunch was killed, and who has continued to work as she did during my wife's lifetime to insure that my home remains orderly and meals are served on time.

My sister Woodie, who is married to an exceptionally fine person, Mr. Jerome "Jerry" Brown, who has never denied her request to return to Atlanta and aid me in my distress. She lived with me for almost a year following my wife's death, and Jerry often visits to help where he can.

The Reverend Joseph L. Roberts, Jr., my pastor and successor at Ebenezer, has been like a son to me, and made my retirement from the active pastorate less difficult than it would have been had his sensitivities not been as sharp as they are. I am satisfied that what we built, in every respect, over the years is in good hands.

Dr. E. A. Jones, one of my Morehouse College professors, who has now retired from the French Department of Morehouse, wrote the first draft of a book about me. I am indebted to him for the time, energy, and love that he put into a work on one whose first days in the French classes were an enormous challenge to Dr. Jones.

Clayton Riley, who assisted me in writing this book.

Ms. Joan Daves, my literary agent, who has shared many pains and pleasures with our family and has shown great patience and business acumen, proving that she is a master of her craft.

Mr. Robert Bender of William Morrow and Company displayed infinite understanding of the complexity involved in the completion of this work.

Mrs. Bernita D. Bennette, another multi-talented person who has been very close to us for more than a decade. Her deep interest in history and research, coupled with her love for and interest in our family, have made her very knowledgeable about the Kings, making her a valuable asset in the completion of my autobiography.

My daughters-in-law, Coretta and Naomi, have been most cooperative and supportive in countless ways as I have worked on my story. They have made it possible to finish many things which would have not been done as they served as resource persons and strong supporters in this endeavor.

My son-in-law, Isaac Farris, Sr., has been of enormous help

and strength from the first days of this writing effort to its completion. He has unselfishly shared his wife with me because he knew she was indispensable to me.

The fine, peerless members of Ebenezer Baptist Church, without whose belief in me and commitment to the quest for freedom, my own journey would have been more difficult. Ebenezians are numbered among God's most special people, and I am happy that we walked together for nearly fifty years.

Dr. Benjamin E. Mays, my good friend of several decades, who read the galleys and accepted the task of writing the Foreword to this book.

The Honorable Andrew J. Young, another tried and true friend, has read the galleys and expressed his thoughts in the Introduction.

And my daughter, Christine, my true support. Quiet, but highly effective, she has been with me through each step of the project, and her critical judgments have been invaluable because her acute perception and probing nature enabled her to read the manuscript and interpret it in a way that no one else could have.

Notwithstanding the assistance that I have received, I know that the final responsibility for this book is mine, and I accept it unreservedly.

—MARTIN LUTHER KING, SR.

Atlanta, Georgia
1980

Introduction

The Reverend Dr. Martin Luther King, Sr., is affectionately known as "Daddy King." I have known and loved Daddy King since I first met him in Ebenezer Church when I came to Atlanta to work with his son, Martin Luther King, Jr., in 1961. I have heard Daddy King preach in that church many times in the years since then, and I have also been present on numerous occasions when he was listening to his son (who was also his co-pastor) preach from the Ebenezer pulpit. When Martin was preaching, Daddy King would often interject, "Make it plain, son! Make it plain!"

Daddy King's sense of urgency that things be made plain is at the heart of this book. Here he makes plain what it was like to grow up in the South in those early days and to fight for justice for himself and for other blacks who wanted to be "free at last." The son of a poor sharecropper in Georgia, Daddy King worked and prayed to get an education and make his mark on the history of his native land.

As a leading Baptist minister and a civic leader, Daddy King has helped to shape the destiny of Atlanta, of Georgia, of the South, and of the nation. His voice has been heard in pulpits and other public platforms across the land, exhorting his fellow Americans to strive fearlessly and tirelessly for freedom and justice. His ministry laid a firm foundation from which his son could build the civil rights movement of the Sixties.

Martin Luther King, Jr., grew up hearing his father preach against the injustices of a segregated society. The dynamic cadences of black Baptist oratory were in his blood. Speaking out against injustice was a way of life in Martin's family. He took it for granted that you didn't let people push you around. He and other Southerners had been hearing these ideas from his father and grandfather, the Reverend A. D. Williams, for many years. When Martin began his own ministry as a very young man with a doctorate in philosophy from Boston University, he might have been regarded with considerable skepticism by black Baptist pastors. Too much education was often threatening to a clergy that had been denied similar opportunity. But he was the son of the Reverend M. L. King, Sr., and this fact bred confidence that he would speak with truth and moreover would be ready to practice what he preached.

Daddy King practiced what he preached. He saw education and economic security as absolute necessities for survival in this world and he preached it as though his law included twelve commandments which black people need to obey for these times: "Thou shalt get thy children to college," and "Thou shalt own thy own home."

It was Daddy King's deep belief in the value of education which set Martin's educational course through Morehouse College, Crozer Seminary, and a Boston University Ph.D. Home ownership was also especially important to the son of a sharecropper. In addition to verbal encouragement, Daddy King also used his influence to assist members of his congregation in the practical aspects of getting together the required amount of money to enter the ranks of homeowners.

Not only members of his congregation but other citizens with problems were always coming to Daddy King for assistance. Whether it was finding a job, or temporary housing. Sometimes it was trouble with school authorities, the police, or lending institutions. It could have been insulting behavior in a store or refusal of treatment at a hospital. People turned to Daddy King for help because they knew that he cared, that he was fearless, and that he would take action. In these confrontations with white power structures, Daddy King would typically start at the top. "I don't want to waste time," he would say. "I need to see the top man. Who's in charge around here?"

Martin Luther King, Jr., grew up seeing his father constantly on the battlefront, standing up for his rights and those of others, and making it plain that he was a child of God who believed in human dignity for himself and for all of God's children. Daddy King's every act of bravery helped to strengthen Martin's own determination to fight fearlessly for freedom and justice.

In these pages you will find evidence of another lifelong theme of this child of a segregated society. "Don't hate," was the message he constantly gave to his congregation and to the members of his family. In spite of all the indignities Daddy King suffered as a child and as a young man, and in spite of all the suffering he endured as the head of a family cut down by the death of both sons and the mother of his children (only his daughter Christine remains), he has refused to let himself be dragged down to hatred. "I love everybody," he often says. "Nobody is going to make me hate."

I was present when he gathered his grandchildren together just after the funeral of his beloved wife, whom we called "Mama King" and whom he called "Bunch." Mama King had been shot down by a psychopath in Ebenezer Church as she was playing "The Lord's Prayer" on the organ. Daddy King had already lost Martin to an assassin's bullet and Alfred Daniel, called A.D., in a drowning accident. Losing his life companion after these other tragedies might have broken a lesser man. But not Daddy King.

Some of his grandchildren were asking, "Why? Why did God let this happen?" In their grief they were trying to make sense out of this latest blow to their family. They called their grandmother "Big Mama." Through the tears the questions came forth. "Why did God let that crazy man kill Big Mama? Why do all these terrible things happen to our family? Why?"

These were hard questions, but Daddy King did not waver in his faith. He let his grandchildren express their bitterness and cry their tears. His counsel to them, however, was clear and unequivocal.

"I know it's hard to understand, but we have to give thanks for what we have left. God wants us to love one another and not hate."

His grandchildren were asking the questions that Job asked, and Daddy King was answering them with the faith of the prophets.

After nearly three hours of family dialogue, during which everyone had a chance to air his or her feelings—Martin and Coretta's four children, A.D. and Naomi's five, and Christine and Isaac Farris's two—Daddy King led everybody in prayer. At the end, he said to them, "Now get out of here, and remember: Don't ever stoop so low that you let anybody make you hate."

Martin Luther King, Jr., was the son of this giant of a man. People will understand Martin better after reading this book about his father. They are hewn from the same mighty oak. Martin grew up in the church, and his whole life was an expression of his sense of ministry—reaching out to the poor and the oppressed, the children of God who needed someone to help them get over into the promised land.

The life of Martin Luther King, Sr., is more than a model which helps to explain the life and ministry of Martin Luther King, Jr. Daddy King's life is a source of inspiration for all of us who join hands in brotherhood, who value integrity, commitment, and courage, and who, like Daddy King, believe that God meant for all of his children to love one another. The task for each of us is to "Make it plain!"

—THE HONORABLE ANDREW J. YOUNG,
   Former Ambassador of the U.S. to the United Nations;
   President, Young Ideas, Inc.

One

"King!"

I can still hear their voices breaking up with laughter and calling out my name in disbelief. Three of my buddies were driving back to Atlanta with me from Jonesboro, Georgia, where we'd all been attending the Atlanta Missionary Baptist Association's annual convention. While guiding my Model T Ford toward the outskirts of the city around one in the morning, I had announced, casually, the name of the young lady I was planning to marry. And this just broke them all up. Here was a green country boy—me—fresh off the farm, who hadn't been living in the city for even a year, telling these three sophisticated young men that he was going to be the husband of Alberta Williams, daughter of one of Atlanta's most prominent and respected ministers, the Reverend A. D. Williams, of Ebenezer Baptist Church.

I had first seen Alberta Williams on Auburn Avenue in Atlanta, a few yards from her home. At that time I was a student at Bryant Preparatory School and she was a boarding student at Spelman Seminary. Miss Williams had recently broken her ankle and was living at home while she recuperated from the fracture; it was while she was taking a walk on her crutches one day that I saw her. When I told my buddies that I'd fallen in love with Miss Williams and planned to marry her, they thought I'd lost my mind or my religion, or both!

"Why, you can't even talk to a refined young woman like that," said T. L. Bracey, who was sitting next to me in the front seat. "With that rough, countrified speech of yours, you might scare the poor woman half out of her wits!"

From the back, James Tisdale and Eddie Cooper threw in their couple of cents' worth. "Now, King," Tisdale chirped in a birdlike voice, "you know God doesn't love ugly, and that's about the worst-looking story I've heard all year—you marrying Alberta Williams. Get on away from here!"

We were all young preachers trying to get started on our careers back there in the summer of 1919, and finding it harder than we ever imagined it could be.

To make ends meet, we took little part-time jobs wherever and whenever we could find them. Mainly, though, we spent our time going to these Baptist conventions, and to revivals, baptisms, camp meetings—anyplace we might have the chance to hear some experienced preachers, or be given a chance ourselves to deliver the Word. We'd teach Sunday school and help out at prayer meetings, trying all the time to acquaint the various congregations around Atlanta with our ability and dedication.

At the time, I owned a Model T in pretty fair condition. That was how my mates and I traveled all around the state, and sometimes over into Alabama or Florida, to learn all we could about the art of Baptist preaching.

We'd gone this particular night to hear a keynote address at the convention. The very highly regarded pastor of Ebenezer Baptist of Atlanta, Reverend Williams, was scheduled to speak, and we all looked forward to hearing the inspiring words he always offered to young churchmen. But the evening had turned out to be a disappointment. Reverend Williams had gone up to Cleveland, Ohio, to look into a possible pastorate for himself there, and he was delayed on his return by a disabled train. He wasn't able to reach Jonesboro in time for the convention and went directly on home to Atlanta. A very young local preacher filled in for him, and got so tongue-tied that he just stumbled and mumbled most of the night away, until somebody had the wisdom to call on one of the choirs to cover up the embarrassment.

By the time Bracey got through with an imitation of this poor guy's mumble . . . erha, that is to say, I, um . . . ah . . . , my car was rocking with laughter all over again. I was into it myself this time. I'd been impressed by one part of this Jonesboro preacher's talk, though. When he mentioned the Reverend Williams's daughter, his voice just seemed to take on a glow as he described her gracious manners, captivating smile and scholarly manner. She was an excellent musician, he went on, and a student at the Spelman Seminary in Atlanta, and she had also organized a fine choir in her father's church.

Well, look out, King, I thought to myself as the fellow was speaking. *Sounds like the woman you been lookin' all over Georgia for!*

So I told my friends I planned to get married to this lovely girl from Atlanta, not bothering to tell them that she'd never met me and wouldn't know me from Adam if she saw me walking past her on the street. But then I figured they didn't need to know everything in the world. Alberta Williams didn't know me . . . yet. But she would, I was sure of it. I'd made up my mind that very night. No doubt about it.

"King," said Eddie Cooper, "you sound like you're absolutely positive about this." Then he started laughing again.

But I was.

I'd arrived in Atlanta with little more than a reputation as a pretty good country preacher. But I soon found out this didn't mean a whole lot in the big city. There were more preachers in Atlanta than anybody could count. I was just one more. Even so, it never did enter my mind that I wouldn't become successful. My greatest strength had always been my confidence, even that part of it I never shared with anyone else but kept carefully and quietly tucked away, deep inside. Even that was shaken up a bit, though, when I started hearing sermons day after day, night after night; enough to realize how stiff the competition really was. A bunch of us were living at this time on a little dead-end street off Auburn Avenue. It's gone now, but in those days there was a big wooden house on that street that belonged to an elderly widow—Mrs. Laster was her name—and she rented rooms to the young, ambitious fellows who seemed to stream into the city constantly, looking to make good. Some did, and a lot didn't. Others stayed for a while, then packed up and went back to the little farm towns they'd left, thinking they were going to conquer the world of cities. For a lot of them, the dream turned out to be bigger, harder, or tougher than they were—too much or much too difficult.

My first few months in the city were often very discouraging. I couldn't say anything, it seemed to me, without someone laughing or correcting my speech.

Down at home, in the country, everybody I ever heard sounded something like me. I never knew how we were mangling the language. But my buddies made sure I found out— and never forgot. Knowing was one thing, though—doing was another. Oh, I tried hard enough, imitating all the smooth talkers I heard around town. But I was so rural that my speech style just ran the English language ragged.

And the fellows living at Mrs. Laster's could ride you, oh, how they could get on your back about anything you didn't know or handle properly. Soon I developed another style—total silence, thinking that I'd escape all their jokes. This didn't work out at all though. If anything, it made them work overtime to get under my skin.

"My, my," Bracey would start off. "I can't speak for the rest of you, but I don't believe I've ever heard of a silent preacher."

"Yes, I hear you, Brother Bracey," Tisdale said in his distinctively high, thin voice. "Seems to me that a young man named King would know just a small amount of the King's English, now wouldn't you think so?"

"Actually," young Cooper'd say, always anxious to get in the last word, "it's very basic, very old, it's been said many times before. You can take the boy out of the country, but Lord knows it's a lot harder to take the country out of the boy."

Now this talk was mostly in fun and had to be taken in that spirit. But it had very serious points about it as well. To be "country" was to be backward, unsophisticated, and hopelessly ignorant. It was true that I had a lot of rough edges, but to my mind they were only temporary. I planned to be as smooth as the most polished people in town. But I really didn't have the first idea just how I was going to accomplish this.

My older sister, Woodie Clara, had lived in Atlanta for about a year when I came up from the farm, and she made one thing very clear to me right away. "There's nothing you can do here without an education, and you might as well get that through your stubborn head, brother, as soon as you can."

Well, she'd hit one nail right on the head. I was stubborn. Thought I knew it all. Preaching was what I did, and I figured I did that pretty well. There was also a notion rolling around my mind that I'd make one mighty fine businessman if I set my sights on that field. And if hard work got it, I'd have a big bank account in no time at all.

"Well, whatever you decide," Woodie cautioned me, "you had better make up that mind of yours to some long hours of book learning. Otherwise, you'll be nothing but another straw in a big wind. . . ."

I resisted all this talk about schooling at first. Why, I'd been the smartest thing ever walked down in the country school I attended as a farm boy. Learned faster and better than anybody.

"You're not *on* the farm, anymore," Woodie reminded me. "This is Atlanta, little brother. Being the smartest here is a whole different matter."

Well, I went on being hardheaded for a while. Found a job, then another, and then an even better one, and every time I made a little money, preaching drifted off a little further from my thoughts, and being a business tycoon crept a little closer.

Fortunately, it didn't take me forever to see just where my hard head was leading me. I was green as the proverbial grass, a backwoods Bible thumper with a gift for a lot of hollering and a little sense. And the more I got around the city the more I was reminded of some sad, aging men I'd grown up watching down in the country. These fellows were preachers in name only, and then only because *they* said they were. Many of them couldn't read, let alone write, and I could recall how they'd shuffle all around towns out there in rural Georgia, carrying a coat-pocket full of pencils they didn't know how to use, trying to impress the local folks with all the "writing" they had to do. Remembering them, it was very hard to see the future. Without so much as half trying I'd end up just like them—coming into town as somebody's guest preacher for one Sunday, then hanging around for another couple of weeks, because they really had no place else to go and, often, no way to get anywhere they wanted to be. God, I wanted more than that.

But it took me a while to understand that wishing wouldn't make it happen. What I wanted, I was going to have to work and work some more to get. And biting off more than one could chew was a ritual being played out every day by those whose reach was so much better than their grip.

So I hitched up my belt and went to work.

As it happened, I was in for a rude awakening. I was then driving a barber-supply truck from dawn till dusk, and my sister Woodie had talked me into stopping in at Bryant Preparatory School, where she was taking classes. Well, I knew I needed that high-school diploma she always talked about—I just didn't feel like taking the time to get it. But I had agreed to take the little tests they gave, and after that I sat down to talk to the registrar.

"Mr. King," he said, "if you want to study here, we'll have to start you in the fifth grade."

I nearly fell off the chair. My twenty-first birthday was only a few weeks away. What on earth would I look like, a great big grown man, sitting in a fifth-grade classroom? No, I couldn't do that, it was asking too much. But Bryant had students much older than I was in even lower grades. At that time—1920—Georgia provided no free education to Negroes beyond the eighth grade; there was not a single high school in the city of Atlanta with a black student enrolled in it. The only way to get that diploma was to pay for your studies.

I wrestled with the idea of whether all of this would be worth it to me, and I told the registrar I'd get back to him. And on my way home with Woodie I argued with her about it. All those years in the country schoolhouse back home hadn't meant a thing, she said. My background was so poor that I was considered almost illiterate.

It was like a pail of cold water thrown right in my face. But finally I said to myself, *Just handle it, King, just go on and do what you need to.*

I started at Bryant School. In the first couple of weeks, my confidence was nearly shattered. It sometimes seemed that I knew practically nothing at all, even at the fifth-grade level. A grown man, out on my own, and I could scarcely read books intended for a ten-year-old child. Bracey had been so right. If I tried to court a young woman like Alberta Williams, Lord, it would be an outright disaster—and now I knew it. But she was on my mind every day of the week. I tried not to think about how long it might take me to finish the courses at Bryant because that only reminded me that Alberta was already studying in college. *Lord, Lord,* I thought.

But nobody had said it was going to be easy, any of this life of mine. So I just went on. After the initial experience of being so embarrassed by the exposure of my ignorance in those class-rooms, I just dug into the work, over and over, working all the time, carrying my books with me wherever I went, reading, going over the lessons until they were ready to pop out of my ears—and then reviewing them all once more just to be certain I knew everything perfectly. I'd sometimes have to drive those barber chairs I delivered out into the smaller towns around Atlanta. All along the way I'd be reciting my lessons to myself. I'd walk down the street practicing my rules of English gram-mar, tangling them all up at times, yelling at myself for being so slow, and getting all kinds of funny stares from folks who just knew I was clean out of my mind. But it didn't matter what anybody thought—except, maybe, *one* person. I had things to get done, and I went about it with all the energy I could find in myself.

Having been so cocky about my "impending marriage," as my mates were calling it, I now had to find a way to meet my bride-to-be for the first time. And it seemed as though the Lord just started putting in a little overtime on my behalf when my sister Woodie told me one afternoon that she was moving from the house of one of our mother's cousins into the very comfortable home of a local minister there in Atlanta.

"You've probably heard of him," she told me. "Reverend A. D. Williams of Ebenezer."

It seemed that the Reverend and Mrs. Williams had decided to take on another roomer when their daughter, Alberta, went off to begin her studies at Spelman Seminary, over on the other side of the city. Rather than have her commute, they decided to let her stay in a dormitory on the campus. In those days, church people were very generous about providing living quarters for young single women, especially those pursuing an education. In the Williams home, a very spacious old Victorian house on Auburn Avenue in Atlanta, there were usually some relatives or boarders being given an opportunity to make themselves at home. The house was neat, and Mrs. Williams and her sister, who lived there too, were known throughout the church community for their fine cooking. I wasted no time telling Woodie how lucky I thought she was to have this opportunity to live in such a fine home, and I encouraged her to stay right there for as long as possible.

Unfortunately, Woodie's being in the Williams house never did give me an opportunity to meet Miss Williams. So I tried walking by her house on my way to the Bryant School, which was then just a few blocks away. I would move as slowly as I could in the hope that Alberta might come out, on her way to church for choir rehearsal . . . anything, it didn't matter, just so I had a chance to talk with her. But mostly I'd see her father out on the porch, relaxing or taking a stretch after dinner, getting some fresh air. I never saw Alberta, though, and I'd just about given up.

Then one evening, she was there. I walked past quickly when I saw her, then turned around and came back. I stood down on the sidewalk, several feet away, and tried to wave just enough to catch her eye. But she never moved. I wondered whether her father was nearby, maybe in the parlor of the house or upstairs in one of the darkened windows, watching every move I made.

Finally I decided I was just going to go ahead with it, and

I walked right on up the pathway to the porch at the front of the house.

She didn't look up for several minutes—at least it seemed that long, perhaps because I wanted to have this chance to exchange a few words with her.

Finally, she glanced up from her book, watched me for a few seconds, then smiled. I guess something began happening right there; she seemed so tiny, and so warm, completely gracious and at ease.

"Hello. You're Reverend King, aren't you? Woodie's talked about you. How pleasant it is to meet you, finally."

Well, I mumbled something back that probably didn't make a bit of sense, I was so tongue-tied. She spoke so well, so clearly, and she put so many words together so well in one sentence, I just couldn't get my answers to stand up and sound right. She asked me about my churches.

"Well, I'se preachin' in two places," I told her, and I thought I noticed her eyes narrow very quickly during the middle of my sentence. Now I knew that I was country, and I figured she knew it too. But I was there and she was, too, so if I was going to say anything to her the way I'd been promising myself I would the first chance I got, well, I was going to have to go right on and sound just as country as I actually was.

"Ain't been here but a short while," I tried to explain. "We from down the country, me and Woodie, an' we got a buncha brothers an' sisters."

For a while she stared. Looked right at me. I could tell she was shy, but she wouldn't flutter her eyes and keep looking away. Just wouldn't. And I liked that. And soon she was smiling again and I felt fine . . . just fine.

I couldn't make a habit of dropping by the Williams house, however, so I had to find some other way to see Alberta Williams. Again, it seemed that the Lord was willing to lend a hand.

Woodie had a friend named India Nelson; she was Alberta's closest friend. That's all I needed to hear. India sometimes went over to Spelman on Sunday afternoons, when the students there could receive guests—it was a very old-fashioned, strict place, where socializing was considered a distraction from a person's studies. Well, India was a friendly sort of person, and I'd often given her and Woodie rides in my car to wherever they might be going, especially on Sunday afternoons.

Finally I got lucky. India asked one day if I'd mind driving her over to Spelman the next Sunday afternoon. She was going to visit Alberta and chat with her for an hour or so, maybe take her some cookies or something that Mrs. Williams had baked. I told India that I'd check my schedule and see if I could get away. Then I rushed back to the rooming house so fast I was out of breath when I hit the door.

Some of the fellows were headed out and asked me to carry them somewhere, but I had other things on my mind, mainly checking on my meager wardrobe to see what I'd wear that Sunday for this momentous occasion. First I knew I'd have to get a couple of boards to put my trousers between, then slip them under my mattress so there'd be a nice crease in them by Sunday. Then I needed to borrow a little lard from Mrs. Laster's kitchen so I could mix it with a little ice water and apply this to the toes of my old shoes to get a good shine started on them. A little lard, a little water, a lot of elbow grease as I buffed and shined, would put them in pretty fair shape in a few days. Then I scrubbed my good shirt so hard I could practically see through the cotton before I put some starch around the collar and asked Mrs. Laster if she could find the time to press it for me.

"Why, Reverend King," she said to me, "you must be fixin' to court some nice young lady . . ."

"No, ma'am," I told her. "I'm fixin' to get married."

Two

I had been a licensed preacher at the age of fifteen. Out in the country, this really wasn't unusual, young boys pursuing rural ministries. It was just a matter of getting a board of deacons at a church to test you on the Bible, then offer you a chance at a trial sermon. Well, I had always been close to church. My mother was a deeply religious woman, and from my very earliest days I was with her at the country services or the many revivals, baptisms, and funerals she attended.

My parents were poor farming people, sharecroppers working the land around Stockbridge, Georgia, when I was born there on the nineteenth of December, 1899. My father, James Albert King, was a lean, tough little fellow, very wiry and strong. As a young man, he'd worked in a rock quarry near town, but lost part of his right hand in an explosion one day. He became quite bitter about this in later years. Quarry work paid fairly good money in those days, more than any Negro was ever going to make farming someone else's land. James King never got so much as a thank-you for the years he put in at that quarry. As soon as he got hurt, they waved him right off the company's property; told him he was through. Nobody'd ever heard of workmen's compensation back then. A man took his chances. If things went wrong for him, the bosses felt no responsibility whatever.

My mother, Delia Lindsay, met my father a short while after his accident. They married there in Stockbridge, and because she was from farming people and never afraid of work a day in her life, the two of them decided to set up housekeeping and work some acres of cotton for a local landowner named Graves. But this man would never do right by my daddy; he and Papa clashed more than once.

There was no way to make any money sharecropping. Owning your mule, maybe a few cows, this was about as much as a farmer working shares could hope to achieve. And even doing this wasn't easy. Whites ruled. A Negro had no rights any white person was bound to respect. If a dispute came up, a man's color was the deciding factor, and a Negro who argued too much or too often was leaning toward his own death. Now, Papa could be hot-tempered, and my mother knew this. She could calm him most of the time when he'd get upset. One of the things that really riled him was a man trying to cheat him in a transaction of one kind or another. Papa gave a hard, good day's work, never shirked, never cut any corners. But to the whites who owned land around Stockbridge, the cotton traders and the tradesmen, there was one set of ethics for themselves and other whites, and another bunch of rules that applied when they were dealing with any black person.

"Cheatin' a nigger," they'd say, "ain't really doin' nothin' wrong. It's like playin' a game, 'cause most times they's too dumb to know the difference anyhow."

To these whites, a Negro wasn't a human being, but just a thing. Our lives were never real as far as they were concerned, and so nothing that might be done to us, no matter how cruel or savage, was real either. My father's bitterness grew out of this kind of atmosphere, which made him into an object instead of a man, and always dared him, under the penalty of being killed, to do anything about it. So he had to walk a tightrope. Once in a while there'd be stories around Stockbridge about "a nigger who's so damn crazy it's better just to leave him alone. No tellin' what the fool might do 'fore we could get to him."

As time went along and my daddy took to drinking a lot of whiskey, as he came to have a look of very quiet but very serious fire in his eyes, more and more people just left him alone, too. A man reaches a point in circumstances like that where he just doesn't care anymore, not about living, not about pain, not about his anger or anything else. Most folks in the country come to learn that it's best to leave a man like this to himself, not to push him too far.

My mother was a different sort of person. She had a temper, too, maybe even worse than Papa's in some ways, because it was so deep in her that anything bringing it out was bringing out some real trouble. But Mama was at peace with herself because of her abiding faith. God's wisdom was the guide in Mama's life, and even in her times of great suffering, which came so many times in her life, she never lost sight of the Lord. No tears could blind her to His presence, and she could not close her eyes so tight in sorrow or in rage that she did not see God's hand reaching out to her. In the worst years, she never surrendered to self-pity or doubt. And over all these years that have passed since I last saw her, my mind and my heart continue to tell me what a remarkable person she was.

Ten children were born to my parents. Nine survived. I was second, right after my sister Woodie; then there was a baby boy, Lucius, who died when he was just a few days old. My father held him so close, Mama told us later, walked that baby around our cabin as the child was burning up with fever. But nothing could be done to save little Lucius, and we lost him. My sisters Lenora and Cleo were born next, about a year apart. Then came three more boys: James, Henry and Joel, who were followed by my two youngest sisters, Lucille, then Ruby, the last of my parents' children.

Through these years, the first of the twentieth century, my mother had babies, worked the fields, and often went during the winter to wash and iron in the homes of whites around town. I look back and wonder where she found the strength to do so much. God, she always told me, provided. Mama said that He gave her all the will to do what was needed. And so I came to admire both of them, the Lord and Mama, for being so able, so strong. But for my mother the rewards of all that she did were not to come in this life. And as I realized this was true, I grew angry inside, never expressing these feelings openly, but carrying them like a huge stone within. Something was wrong, I knew, when someone who tried so hard, who kept her faith, and who provided so much of a sense of the righteous path for all her children, came away, finally, with so little for herself.

As a boy I was called Mike King. Mama always insisted that she'd named me Michael, after the archangel, and Papa was just as adamant about saying that I was Martin Luther, after two of his brothers. Mike was kind of a compromise. Mama didn't like it all that much, and she always called me Michael, but Papa said he didn't *mind* Mike, and since all my young friends referred to me by that name, he never objected.

It's fair and truthful to say that I was always a little closer to my mother than my father. Papa and I had a somewhat difficult relationship on many counts. Mama would take me to every church service she attended, and I think he always resented this a little. I was the first son, he expected me to follow in all of his footsteps, be just like him on almost every point. But Papa was a farmer. More specifically, he was a sharecropper, which meant he was locked into a kind of work he hated, a kind that could take him nowhere but in the endless circle that was governed by the seasons: spring planting, fall harvesting, turning over new ground through the winter, waiting for the following spring. It was a life he never was able to escape. I would escape it, eventually, and sometimes it seemed to me that he wanted all of his children, certainly all of his sons, to stay out there with him, growing old on somebody else's land, just waiting to die.

Church was a way to ease the harsh tone of farm life, a way to keep from descending into bitterness. Even before I knew what the Christian faith was all about, or even understood the rituals and the ceremonies, church music had made a very deep impression on me. As a small child, I started singing, and soon was being taken by my mother to the revivals and other services, where people spoke of little Mike King, who could sing so well, and who loved church with all his heart. It was true. I always felt extremely happy and completely at ease within the church setting; I never tired of going to the revivals, the baptisms, weddings, all the gatherings where people would be found bearing a particular witness.

Papa was not religious, and although I don't think he was very enthusiastic about my attending so many church affairs, he never interfered with Mama's taking me.

I developed a strong voice and could sing nearly any song after hearing it just a few times. Few of the country folks played or even had any church instruments except guitars, and some churches didn't allow them to be played because they were used to celebrate the devil's music—or so some folks were convinced. The human voice was the rural church's organ and piano. And when the traveling preachers came through the small Georgia towns, they were sure to make an impression if they could sing well. The traveling preacher, sometimes called the Country Circuit minister, or C.C. Rider because in some areas he traveled by horseback, built a word-of-mouth reputation on an ability to cite the Scriptures—usually from memory, because not many of the country folks had ever learned to read. He also helped his own cause among the people if he could bring some music to the service.

I grew up in this tradition of rural Baptist worship, respecting and loving it. The more folks asked me to participate in services, the more I responded. My singing often brought congregations to a peak of emotional fervor, but I never felt I was losing control of any of these crowds of people. And at these services that I attended, so many of the old-time preachers, who could recite Scriptures for hours on end, provided me with a great sense of the gestures, the cadences, the deeply emotive quality of their styles of ministry. And when I was alone, I would try to duplicate the things I heard them do, and having a good memory for songs and the parts of the Bible that were especially popular among country folks, the Psalms, for example, I soon was experiencing a growing personal vision of spending a life in the ministry myself.

At Floyd Chapel, my mother's church, the board of deacons had always frowned on the licensing of very young preachers. I could see that even in the years to come there would be resistance to my responding to the call I was now experiencing.

That call didn't come all at once, in any single place or at any one time. It built as an ever-deepening experience that I could not deny, even though I was so young, so unprepared to understand all of this.

When I was ten, there was a certainty growing in me. By that time I was the match of any church singer around. My voice did not ever grow tired; I could literally sing all afternoon and late into the night.

But I hated the country life almost from the time I was able to stand and walk around by myself. The farm work itself wasn't so bad, I could handle that better than most folks who claimed they loved it. It was the world all around that work, this is what tore me up inside.

Of course, none of this came about naturally. I was taught, day by day, night after night, just why the place I lived in was a place I'd grow up wanting to get away from the first chance I got. As a small kid, I had a friend, Jay was his name, and we'd walk around together, just looking over the countryside, chunking rocks across creeks to see which one of us could make one skip the farthest, racing along those dusty old Georgia roads to see who ran the best, or who could climb highest in a tree or catch a ball made out of tied-up old rags better than anybody in Stockbridge or maybe in the whole state of Georgia. We had a lot of fun, never fought, never argued too much. One day we were laughing about something along the railroad tracks that ran through town, and we came upon Jay's father and some other men sitting near the depot. One of these farmers nudged Jay's dad and asked him, "Who's that with Jay?" And Jay's father answered, "Oh, that's just one of my niggers. . . ." The words just reached inside and twisted at me. Jay had a name, he always did. I didn't. Sometimes I was Mike, but around these men I was somebody's nigger. I was six, maybe seven years old at the time. I've never forgotten. It was a beginning of many understandings. There would be more.

A man was killed one afternoon on a road just outside the center of Stockbridge. Some men from over at the mill had gotten their pay and started drinking some corn liquor from down in a still near there. As often was the case when some of the tongues of these folks got loosened up a little, there was a lot of talk about niggers. The politicians had been stumping through the area for several weeks before this, and it was a basic tactic of these officeholders—or those who were running for office—to stir up the passions of all potential voters by appealing to their sense of insecurity. Things were rough for everybody in Georgia at this time, no matter their color. Cotton was down to where you practically had to pay somebody to take it off your hands. Other crops had been eaten up by a very harsh winter. The politicians would come through and find people screaming at them for letting the voters down. And the politicians would come back: "Hell, neighbors, it's not our fault. If it wasn't for all these damn niggers, the whole world would be a lot better off!"

Now the mills around town always had a few Negroes working at one kind of job or another. If you were black, though, the only thing that made it all right for you to have a job was that you were paid less than the whites. In some places that was law. It was the custom everywhere. Well, on this day, a Negro from the same mill as the men who were sitting around drinking passed along the road, counting the little bit of money he'd made that week.

One of the whites yelled out that this was the reason there were so many decent white men out of work, too many niggers around taking away their jobs. Well, the black man said nothing. He tried to smile his way past these men, because it was too late for him to turn and go the other way. So he just tried to grin his way by. I had been out playing in the woods, and was running on home for supper.

"What the hell are you laughin' at, nigger?" I heard one of the mill men shout. I stopped. Then I saw the black man down the road a piece, starting to walk real fast. They went after him. "Nigger," one of them screamed, "I asked you somethin'."

"Naw, suh," the man said. "I ain' laughin'. Jus' on ma way home is all . . ."

"Commere, nigger!"

"I ain' laughin', suh, honest I ain't."

"Nigger come struttin' down the road like he thinks he's up North someplace. Pocket full of money. Laughin' at white folks!"

They tried to take his pay from him and a little tussle started. The Negro was a pretty good-sized fellow, and he put up a struggle. "This's money fo' my chil'ren now. I cain' let you have that." One of the mill men ran and got a tree branch, just ripped it down, and while some of the others held this fellow, the man from the mill started to beat him about his head with the big branch. Blood started pouring out of the man's mouth and he started to fall. It seemed like all their feet started kicking him, then, with those heavy boots the men at the mill wore. The man started crying out in pain, and I suddenly realized I was so terrified that I was unable to move. The mill men began dragging him toward me, and for a moment I thought I was going to pass out. They pulled him right on past me—it was as if I hadn't even been there watching. As they went by I could see through all their arms and legs, I could see the man's head covered with blood, slack against his shoulder. Suddenly these men from the mill were whooping like crazy as one of them took off his belt and wrapped it around the Negro's neck. They all lifted him up and tied the end of the belt to this tree and let him go. . . .

I was still there when they'd all gone staggering off down the road, laughing to themselves, waving the jugs of corn whiskey they carried. The black man was dead, his head all twisted over, his feet about five or six inches off the ground. Suddenly I could hear my breathing coming through me harder and harder, and then there was a scream pouring through my lips that nobody heard but me. The man was dead, just a few feet in front of me, and all I could think about was that he had probably died before they even put him up on that tree. *Why*, I thought, *why did they do that?*

But, of course, I had no answers. It was too complicated, then. All I could do was to run on home, keep silent, never mentioning what I'd seen to anyone, until many, many years later, when I understood it better.

And when that did happen, when I did tell what I'd seen, it would be in the last days before I left home for good, to go and live in Atlanta. And what I had come to understand, as I told my mother, was that I'd carry a hatred in me for white people until the day I died. I would hate every one of them and fight them day and night, trying my best to destroy any of them I had a chance to. These feelings began to settle into my heart and I didn't know any reason they should be rooted out. Whites, I felt, would never be able to change because they didn't know how, they would never develop the capacity to be another kind of people. For so long had they lived with their doctrine of white supremacy that the feelings of superiority that resulted were not ever going to be rooted out. I realized very early that self-protection was a strong force in all human beings. My way to protect myself, I thought, was to build around myself an armor made of my hatred for whites. It was needed. It was valuable. And it helped me to deal with the memories, the terrible dreams and recollections. To hate those responsible made it bearable, and so I indulged myself, and began to despise every white face I saw.

By now, I *hated* farming. Papa knew it, and my mother sensed it, too, though she tried to keep me from expressing my feelings about the matter quite so openly. I think she questioned my having such passionate feelings at so early a point in my life.

Mama often cautioned me about being premature in my determination to make my life over into something new, something I had not approached carefully with thoroughness and some caution. Life didn't run on a single track like those old country railways; it had detours, changes, alternating routes, complete stops at times.

But as I was nearing my teens, everything began to take on a very solid shape. At least I thought so. I seemed to be seeing everything clearly. Perhaps I had a tendency to oversimplify.

There's more to preaching than breath and britches, country folks would say. But I felt very secure in my calling and my faith. The warm embrace of the church surrounded me wherever I went. There was simply no other place for me. But there were events in my life that would shape my decision to seek the pulpit. And the years beginning with my twelfth birthday turned out to be extremely important in that decision.

I faced some painful moments during that time. Uncertainty was often with me. Doubts crept in on me, and although I was able to shake them off, the impressions left were not so easily dismissed. Even today, when more than seventy years have gone by, I think of my parents, out there in Stockbridge, and all they confronted in life that made my leaving there both so difficult and so very necessary.

A neighbor of ours had an ailing cow one spring. The poor animal couldn't give milk and was just mooing and lowing all the time, bleary-eyed, ready to pass on any day. Mama was always a believer in the redeeming value of sharing however little we might have with those even less fortunate, so one morning she filled a bucket with milk, set a large chunk of butter floating in it, and sent me to carry it over to this neighbor. It was a beautiful sunny day in the early summer, and heading there I had to pass the local sawmill. I stopped to watch the work going on there, the oxen grunting loud as they hauled huge logs up from the forest, the men driving the animals forward toward the mill, which was on a slight incline a few hundred yards from a stream that flowed through the woods. As I watched, a man approached me, and I recognized him as the millowner. He was well on in years and had a reputation for being hard and mean when he wanted to be, which was most of the time.

"Say, boy," he called to me, "run get a bucket of water for my men from down at the stream."

As politely as I knew how, I told him I was doing an errand for my mother, and I had to be moving on. Well, this just infuriated him. Before I could move, he grabbed my shirt and pulled me toward him. I started struggling to get away, and the shirt tore all to pieces. He kicked the bucket of milk and butter from my hand, spilling everything over the ground. I was so frightened about what Mama would do to me for not getting to this neighbor what she'd sent that I actually reached down to try and scoop the butter back into the bucket.

The millowner kicked me. His boot thudded against my ear and sent me falling over backward. He was coming after me again when I managed to scramble back up on my feet, just in time to feel his fist smash against my mouth. I fell down again, so dizzy now I could scarcely see. The voices of other men filtered into the haze that was rapidly taking over my senses, and when I could see at all, someone had lifted me up to my feet. Some of the millworkers were holding the owner, and the man who'd helped me up was yelling to me to take off and get on home or wherever I was going. There was blood on my face now, but I refused to cry. This I couldn't do, even though my head was aching. . . .

But there were tears in my eyes when I finally reached our little cabin several minutes later. Papa was out in the fields and wouldn't be home until after dark. Mama was in the front yard with the girls, washing clothes in a big iron tub they had set down over a fire. The girls jumped away when they saw me, and Mama took one look and dropped all the clothes she had and rushed over to me.

"Who did this to you, Michael?" she asked, her voice very low and tight. "Who was it?"

I was too shaken up to speak and just stood there, trembling over the thought of Mama whipping me for not getting my errand finished. "*Michael!*" she screamed. "*Who did this?*"

Moments later we were retracing my steps back to the mill. Mama had a grip on my wrist that squeezed like an iron vise, and I'd never in my young life seen a look in her eyes as cold, as furious as the one that was there now. When we reached the mill, I tried to pull back away from her. The millowner was standing right out in front of the place, laughing with some of his men about the lesson he'd taught that "smart-ass little nigger."

Mama pulled me along with her and stopped right in front of him. The men around the millowner stopped laughing. They looked from me to my mother and then to the millowner. He had a big grin spread out all over his face. Mama stared straight into his eyes.

"Did you do this to my child?" she asked. My torn shirt was hanging loose off my shoulders, and the blood was drying around my mouth.

"Woman!" the millowner yelled. "You lost your mind? Get the hell outta here before I—"

"Did you do this to my child!" Mama screamed.

"Yeah," the millowner answered. "And so what about it? You got somethin' to say? What is it?"

I had never seen my mother move so quickly. She leaped at this man, dug her shoulder into his middle and knocked him back against the side of the mill shed. My mother had worked all of her life, she was powerfully built and had the strength of any man. The millowner was shocked. He tried to grab hold of her, but she tripped him up and he fell to the ground. Oh, Lord, what did he do that for? Mama jumped down on him, pounding away at his face. Some of the mill hands tried to get her off the man, but she punched one of them right in his mouth so hard he spun around and stumbled back, looking as if he'd never been hit that hard in his life. The millowner pushed and turned, but he couldn't get Mama off him. She raised up and brought both her fists down across his nose, and blood spurted out of his face all over the ground. Then she got up. The other men had moved back a little. She stared at them. Her eyes were like coals blazing out of their sockets.

"You can kill me!" she shouted. "But if you put a hand on a child of mine, you'll answer."

She stood her ground and the millowner got to his feet, watching closely as Mama balled up her fists again. But the man just pointed at us. "Get off my land. Next time you come around here, we'll see who answers. Now git!"

I was scared somebody would pull out a gun and shoot us down. But Mama knew better. Too many people had seen how it all had happened. The only way the millowner could live it down was just to say no more about it, just let it go. He sure didn't want it around that a farm woman had come up to his mill and whipped him in a fair fight. He knew none of his workers were going to say anything. They had their jobs to think about. So when Mama pulled me away from the mill, I think most of the people there just wanted to pretend that what they'd seen had never happened.

Mama cleaned off my face when we got back home and had my sister Woodie hold a cool, damp cloth against the bruise near my mouth. "If your papa asks you," said Mama, "you just tell him you got to playin' and fell down, you hear, Michael?"

Then she explained to me that any talk about this could mean death. And I knew she was serious. I knew that Negroes had been killed for a lot less. I carried a memory of this.

But word of this man's hurting me somehow did get to my father. He lost control of himself, grabbed his old rifle from above the door of our cabin, and rushed off to the mill. Mama couldn't stop him; he just brushed her aside. That was the last we saw of Papa for several months, and the very first time I saw, firsthand, the face of a mob. That night, some men on horses came riding up to our place with rifles in their hands. Mama sent us all into hiding behind the cabin. She talked to them, and we heard one of the men say that Papa had come over to the mill and vowed to shoot the man who'd touched his son. But the millowner wasn't there and Papa left. Somebody told him, before he could get back home, that a group of men in Stockbridge were gathering up to get him. He didn't want any shooting around us, and he took off into the woods, carrying his rifle with him in case anybody followed.

The men rode off, but one of them, an uncle of my old friend Jay, came back out the next morning and told me to get a message to my father. "Tell him to stay out of sight until this all blows over. They'll forget all about it in a few months, but there could be some danger to him in the meanwhile."

We lived in great fear for the next weeks. Food was very scarce, and we were advised not to go into the commissary, a company store operated by the Cotton Trade, while this *heat* was still hanging in the air.

A little over six weeks went by, and one night I heard Papa, whistling the way he'd taught me one day while he was taking my brothers and me hunting. I recognized it right away, got up from my bedroll, and ran out to the woods to see him.

"Why didn't you tell me that man hit you?" he asked me.

"Mama told me not to say anything, that it could mean death, Papa."

"I'm gonna blow one of these crackers' heads off before I leave here," Papa told me. There was whiskey on his breath.

"Papa, my friend Jay's uncle said this all gon' blow over soon if you just stay outta sight. Told me to say you should give it all time to cool down. . . ."

He hated running from them. I could see it as he spoke. Little by little they took pieces of his life away from him, and now they took him away from his kin. He was fighting every day, I realized, with no rest at all. And I was so afraid they'd kill him, I started to shake all over.

"Keep still!" shouted Papa. "You lookin' out for things?"

"Tryin', Papa."

"You better," he told me. "You just better." We sat there in the night for several minutes more. Then Papa got up, and without another word he disappeared back into the woods.

Mama was feeling poorly when fall came around. My brothers and sisters worked with me; we all did the best we could, but we just weren't experienced enough to handle the farm, and things sank down a long way. A deep chill was in the air when Papa finally did come on back. He couldn't save much, though. The cotton turned out bad. We hardly got pennies for it. We picked the vegetables too late, and most of them spoiled. Papa just stayed angry at us, and started drinking more and more. He and Mama argued a lot now. Every day there was something to start him yelling at her. Whenever he left the house, he carried his rifle along, but he didn't take any of us with him. My brother Joel was about the best shot around Stockbridge, but Papa left him home, and went out by himself. With all that whiskey in him, he couldn't see to hit anything. There was hardly any rabbit or any other meat in the house after that. And whenever Papa got back, he was staggering from his liquor.

When the mill incident was finally over with, Jay's uncle was the one who came out and told us. Things had kind of eased back to normal, he said. I wondered just what was normal for us, and how long we could expect it to last.

Three

On those farms in Georgia when I was growing up, a child was always looked upon first as a worker, then as a youngster. The large family was a rule much more than it was an exception. Many hands were needed to complete the hard, constant work that was so central to life in the country. As a result, school became a luxury around Stockbridge. I don't remember going for more than three months during any single year. An old shack had served for more years than anyone could remember as the school for Negro kids, and there was one teacher for all of us, young ones and older alike. The wife of Floyd Chapel's preacher, Mrs. Low, taught us, working as hard as one person could to bring us an education in that cold and damp little building. We had no books, no materials to write with, and no blackboard for her to use in instructing us. But I loved going, particularly when we began learning numbers, which always had a fascination for me.

Mama was very encouraging so far as my schooling was concerned. Although she'd never learned to read or write herself, there was a great sense of the value of learning within her. She was just the opposite of my father in this respect. He never saw the value of education. And he made going to school difficult for me by insisting I carry out all my chores early in the morning before I left the house, during those periods, mainly in the winter, when Mrs. Low taught her classes. So I got up early, fed chickens and pigs when we had them, carried water, got firewood. I saved my favorite chore for last—currying the mule. I loved animals, and so this part of the work was something I actually looked forward to, even with my eyes still half shut on all those chilly, dark winter mornings. It was a mule, in a roundabout way, that gave me one of my very first true tests of self-confidence at school. All the other kids teased me constantly. They'd see me currying our mule near our shed first thing every morning, and by the time I reached the school yard, the guys who knew me would be chanting stuff like, "Here comes the fool, he smells just like a mule!" And I put up with it. The mule did have a way of clinging to me long after I'd left him. But one day when I'd had enough of all this chanting, when they'd even gotten some of the girls to join in, which *really* upset me, I just yelled back: "Hey, I may smell like a mule, but I sure don't think like one!"

They shut up. No more chants were heard for a good while.

It was at school, small and broken down as it was, that I learned of the world beyond the farm. Mrs. Low told stories as a way of keeping our attention, and she was very good at it. My imagination just began to soar when she talked about big cities and even bigger countries, trains that traveled across the whole country, not just past Stockbridge on the way to Macon. I wanted to go to one of those cities and stay. I memorized all the places she talked about. And when she talked about numbers and planets, and other times in history, I learned everything by heart. I'd walk around saying the multiplication tables, doing long division as I made it up, humming the lessons, saying them over and over as I ran through the woods playing or just walking home from school.

Soon all I was thinking about was leaving the country, becoming a teacher myself, or a builder, or a railroad engineer—anything that would get me away.

Sometimes I shared these dreams with Mama. She'd laugh and tell me not to run off and leave without telling her first.

It was hard to think about it all, though, wanting to go away from there and find another kind of life. How could I go and leave my mother behind?

"Michael," she'd say, "if you have to leave this place, you just go right on and leave, you hear? When the time comes, and you're grown, don't you worry about anything. Go on and live your life, son."

How could I do both, though, I'd find myself thinking. Make Mama happy, and myself, too? And then I'd think, *When you get older, these things work themselves out in some grown-up way.* I knew they'd work themselves out for me, too, just as Mama said: *When the time comes . . .*

One harvest, when I was about twelve years old, Papa finally gave in to my pleading with him to take me to the Cotton Trade for that day when he got payment for his crop. I'd never been before; this was grown-folks' business, Papa always told me; more than that, it was man's business. "Well," Papa said, "all right. This time." He figured, I guess, that a twelve-year-old was ready to see some of the ways of the world. So we jumped on his wagon and rode on into Stockbridge with the last part of our cotton crop. I was very excited about seeing all those people and all the transactions that would be taking place. And I knew that my head for numbers was a whole lot better than Papa's. He'd probably thank me for helping him add everything up as fast as I knew how to do by that time.

We got to the Cotton Trade, and Old Man Graves, the man who owned the land we lived on, waved Papa on over to the scales, told him to bring the rest of our crop over for the final weighing process that would determine how much my father had earned for all that work he'd done over the year.

As we started over, Papa looked down at me beside him on the wagon and said, "Boy, you just watch and listen and keep your mouth shut."

I figured he wanted me to learn as much as I could and not miss anything by talking too much. But there was a lot more to his warning, as I soon found out.

Graves was known to the farmers and the traders as "Settle Up," the man who gave you the price for your cotton and paid you. He also ran the commissary, where you bought tools and supplies, and he kept the books on how much everybody owed in there, because that amount would be subtracted at the end of each harvest from the money a man had coming for his crops. All the figures were kept by "Settle Up," his word was the final one on every business deal. Nobody—and especially nobody who was black—could go against him without getting into serious trouble.

Papa unloaded the wagon along with some of Settle Up's men, and they checked to see how much he'd brought in already. It usually took a few trips to bring everything down to the Cotton Trade on those little wagons we had, but I'd watched my father put everything on each trip before he left our place, and I'd been keeping track of just how much he'd brought in.

Well, all these men around the scales and the loading platforms got to joking and laughing with Papa. "Jim," they'd say, "why, boy, you done right well this year. Got you a few dollars comin'; what you gon' do with all that cash? Get good an' drunk, I'll bet!" Everybody was laughing, and Papa just smiled a little and went on about his business. I could feel something all around, something that didn't feel too good to me. I wasn't sure what it was, I just didn't feel that things were going the way they should. But I remembered what my father had told me about watching and listening. There was plenty I could learn if I kept my eyes and ears open.

Old Man Graves, "Settle Up," weighed my daddy's cotton and told him how much money he had coming; it was around thirty dollars. "Papa," I said . . .

"Now, you just hush up, boy!" he whispered to me. He went over and got his slip from the commissary, which showed how much he owed there, and came back to "Settle Up." "Mr. Graves," he said, "I b'lieve my bill over to the commissary leaves me a small piece of money comin'."

"Settle Up" smiled. "Why, you did right good this year, boy," he told my father. "Tell you what I'm fixin' to do. 'Bout time you had a chance at that bottomland out by the sawmill. It's yours, Jim boy, start on it quick as you can."

I was standing with Papa's wagon and mules. A few of the other farmers around me started to get restless. "Come on,

"Settle Up," they shouted. "Give that nigger what he got comin'. There's white folks here to tend to business, you know."

"Settle Up" reached into his pocket and counted out eighteen dollars for my daddy, which was what he was supposed to get after the man at the commissary totaled up what Papa owed for the year.

"Papa," I said again.

"Boy, I told you to keep quiet!"

"But Papa," I finally was able to call out to him, "ain't nothin' been said 'bout the cotton seed!"

Suddenly, everything and everybody got quiet. Even the horses and the mules, the dogs that had been running all around, just seemed to stop and stand quietly.

"Boy," my father snapped at me, "what did I tell you to do?"

I looked past him to the platform where "Settle Up" stood. The veins on his neck seemed like they were about to pop right out. His face was turning beet-red. "You better get that sassy little nigger outta here, Jim," he said to my father, "'fore I kick his little butt!"

My father stiffened. He looked up at "Settle Up" and said, very quietly: "Naw, Mr. Graves, it can't be like that, now."

"Settle Up"'s eyes got big. "What?" he roared at my father, who just stared the man right back in the eye.

"Don't nobody touch my boy, Mr. Graves. Anything need to be done to him, I'll take care of it."

Graves jumped down from his platform and stepped right up next to my father. "Who the hell you think you talkin' to, nigger?" he said.

Papa never backed up an inch, and when he spoke he was looking "Settle Up" right in his face. "Only thing I'm sayin', Mr. Graves, is nobody puts a hand on my boy. If there's some reason you need to know that, then I s'pose it's you I'm tellin'."

Some of the other men moved over and formed a little circle around Papa and "Settle Up."

Now Graves was a big, beefy fellow whose fists looked like a couple of hams hanging down from his wrists. But I could see that Papa wasn't about to back off from him, and it looked like there'd be some trouble. I'd heard men say that my father could handle himself awfully well in a fair fight. He didn't have a lot of size going for him, but he was quick, and those lean arms were like steel rods. He could hit hard. Graves had been cheating everybody for years; the white farmers around Stockbridge had had bad dealings with him, too, and as they gathered around Papa and the old cotton trader, it seemed as though they all had the scent of blood pushing them forward. They wanted to see a fight, this was clear enough. Whoever won it didn't matter, they'd have some satisfaction either way. "Settle Up" could see right away that nobody was really on his side, and a few of his so-called friends among those whites who formed a circle around him and Papa would have liked nothing better than to see the man, white as he was, put right down on his rump by a Negro smaller than he.

I was getting scared. I could feel my heart pounding harder and harder in me. Papa motioned for me to go over by the wagon with the mules, and I knew he meant for me to stay there no matter what happened. So I started off, but turned back after a few steps and called back to him: "Papa, don' forget that ain' nothin' been said yet 'bout the cotton seed!"

Well, this broke some of that tension, because the next thing I knew the whites were just laughing away about me, saying I was nothing but "a crazy little nigger don' know how to keep his mouth shut!" But I think, too, that some of them had sons, and they wanted to believe that their own boys would speak up by their sides when they needed them to.

"Gon' pay that nigger fer 'is seeds, 'Settle Up,' " I heard someone yell as I was walking to the wagon. "Quit cheatin' on what you owe!"

This started a roar from the rest of the men standing around. "Pay the nigger!" they shouted. "Pay 'im, pay 'im!"

Well, "Settle Up" turned beet-red. He looked around. Papa hadn't moved an inch. I looked over there from my place by the wagon and all of a sudden here was "Settle Up" with a big grin on his face.

"Aw, hell, I wasn't 'bout to cheat nobody. Them seeds just slipped my mind is all. I'm gonna pay this boy, pay him everything I owe him!"

Well, of course, hearing this just made my heart leap I was so happy. And my joy just rose further when "Settle Up"'s men weighed all our bales of cotton seed. Altogether we'd brought in eighteen bales to the Cotton Trade. I saw "Settle Up" go in his little office and come back out with a huge handful of cash. "Boy," he said to Papa, "ya seed is worth ninety dollars a bale. Here's ya money."

And he stuffed all that cash down into my father's hand. Lord, I just couldn't believe it, that much money. This made me so happy I could hardly stand still. Papa was very quiet. He just took the money and thanked "Settle Up," then turned and started to our wagon. "Come on, son," he said to me.

As we rode home, I got a strange feeling. Papa looked so angry, his fists all tightened up, his mouth set mighty hard in his face.

"Papa," I said to him . . .

But he interrupted me right away. "Shut up, boy!" Before I realized just how angry he was I started to say something else, and he reached over the seat of the wagon and cuffed me so hard on the head I nearly fell off.

"I told you, damn it! I told you to keep ya mouth shut."

Well, of course, I wasn't able to understand. It just didn't make any kind of sense to me. All that money Papa'd gotten, that "Settle Up" was trying to cheat him out of. But maybe I hadn't really listened carefully enough. If I had, the memory of "Settle Up" 's words to my father as we pulled away from the Cotton Trade on our wagon would have stuck clearly in my mind.

"Boy," he said to Papa, "I'm gon' see from now on that you get everything you got comin'. I'm gon' see to it personally. . . ."

As the sun was coming up the next morning, I heard voices outside in our front yard. My youngest sister, Lucille, was tugging at my arm, trying to wake me and saying that there were men near our cabin "fussin' with Papa."

I peeked through the doorway and saw Papa. Beyond where he was standing, toward the road to town, "Settle Up" and some of his men from the Cotton Trade had taken the mule and some tools Papa had been paying on at the commissary. "You got till tonight, nigger," "Settle Up" yelled at Papa, "to get you and the rest of your people off my land!"

Papa tried to talk him out of it, but "Settle Up" wasn't listening. The bottomland Papa had been promised was going to be worked by somebody, "Settle Up" said, "who won't give me so much damn trouble."

Now I understood why Papa hadn't been so pleased about the seed money. It came with a heavy price. By later in the afternoon we were packed up and off those acres that "Settle Up" owned. We put everything that would fit into the wagon. But the mule belonged to him. He had taken it with him when he and his men left. All we could do was push on down toward town and wait. The look on Papa's face told me we were in trouble. He was in pain. For getting only what was right, what was due him, he now had to get off the shares he'd been working. His family was without a home. What did being "right" mean, I wondered, if you had to suffer so much for it?

While we camped out there along the road for the next few days, Papa went around in town, seeing if another one of the landlords would give him some cotton shares to work. They all refused. "Settle Up" had talked to them. He knew how to get back at folks who crossed him. And he could put pressure on those who were in debt to him. Papa wasn't able to find any land to work. He'd go off and get drunk. It didn't take long for that piece of money I "helped" him get for the seeds to dry up.

One of the white property-owners Mama and Woodie had washed and ironed clothes for sent us word that there was a little shack on a corner of their land, and we could move in there. Every day, it seemed, Papa found some reason to yell at me, get on me no matter how much I tried to help out. Nothing I did was right. Mama asked him to ease up, but he shouted her down. My sisters, especially Ruby, were too young to understand what was going on: the outdoors all the time, the waiting, and finally the moving into a new place.

Woodie was just getting into her teens, and the woman she and Mama worked for urged us all to move into the city. She told Mama to get us all in school there, especially Woodie, who was proving to be a very bright young woman. Papa couldn't say anything while the woman was around, but as soon as she wasn't, he'd start yelling at Mama to quit listening to all that foolishness about schooling for all of us. The farm was good enough for him, it was good enough for his kids. Mama said very little. But I could feel her wanting Woodie to go where she could have a better chance in life than doing someone else's housework was ever going to provide.

Papa was drinking more and more. Slowly, steadily, he was falling apart. His work fell off. He forgot things he was supposed to do, broke up tools when he got mad, and stayed away from the little shack we had moved into. He'd be gone for days at a time. When he came back he'd be yelling and ordering everybody around with threats. My young brothers and sisters grew more and more afraid of him. From the look in Woodie's eyes, I saw that she was just waiting for the day to come when she'd be able to leave. I felt the same way.

All that really interested me now was getting the deacons at Floyd Chapel to give me a chance at a trial sermon. I wanted my preacher's license, even though I wasn't yet fourteen. But the deacons told everybody they weren't going to give me a chance to be tested, not yet anyway. Folks in the church were starting to grumble about this, telling the deacons to let me preach. But they kept holding out, making up one excuse after another—they couldn't get a full deacon board meeting together to decide, Reverend Low was away and couldn't give his approval—just one stumbling block after another.

I always thought that jealousy was at the bottom of that attitude the deacons had about me. I could read, whereas most of them didn't know the alphabet. So they kept me coming back to take their little tests on the Bible. But even then, as a boy, I knew more than all of them put together. Finally, the deacons passed me. I was licensed. And I went on out to preach.

The only thing wrong during this whole period was that Papa picked at me every chance he got, making fun, laughing, cussing and calling me names.

He walked into the house on this particular night, and we could all tell he had himself full of whiskey; he was barely able to walk up the path to our door. Usually we just tried to stay out of his way when he was like that, the way, I guess, that millions of people do in families with drinkers. But he was in a bad mood, and I could see a look of concern come across my mother's face. She shushed some of the younger ones, Ruby, Lucille, my brother James, they were all just little at this time, and Mama finally told me to take them on outside in the fresh air while it was still early. Papa just looked around at everybody, his eyes half shut, his mouth loose. I could feel trouble moving in the house. He was in an ugly disposition.

I could hear the kids out in the yard playing, and then Mama began humming the way she generally did when she was cooking or at some other chore. Otherwise the house was quiet.

Papa had a big fish, wrapped up in a newspaper, tucked under his coat. He pulled it out.

"Delia," he said, his words unsteady, "I want this fish for supper, want you to cook it for me right now."

Mama kept stirring this little pot she had on the wood stove.

"James Albert," she said, in a very steady voice, "I already started supper for the children."

He leaned close to her. "Woman," he said, "I told you I want this fish. Now you cook it!"

Mama turned around and looked him close in the face.

"I am cookin' supper, James Albert!"

He must have seen something in her that said she wasn't going to back away from what she had to do. Papa stared for a moment, then pulled his hand back suddenly and slapped her in the face.

I was on my feet as Mama reeled back away from him and tried to raise her arms to protect herself. He moved after her. I caught up to him as he raised his hand at her again, and I pulled him around to face me. His eyes seemed to be swimming around in his head, he was weaving, but I could feel the strength that man had in his arms, in his hands. My papa was tough, no question about it.

"Don't you hit my mama," I said to him. "Don't you hit her no more, Papa, I ain't gon' let you."

His eyes began squinting at me. "You ain't gon' *what?*" he said. "Boy, I'll knock you into next week!"

He swung the other hand at me, and I was knocked back off of him, but I held on to his other hand and pulled him away from Mama. We started wrestling across the room, crashing against the table and into the walls. God, he was a strong man. Even with all that liquor in him, I had my hands full. By this time in my young life I was built like one of these blocking backs in football. I was a little on the stubby side, but with big shoulders and a lot of hard meat on me. It wasn't just a father and his son going round that shack, but two strong country men looking to hurt one another.

I finally got a grip around his neck and held on to him while I told Mama to go on out and leave us. She was still over against the wall beside the stove where he'd hit her. She didn't move.

Papa fell underneath the weight I'd been pressing on him and I was able to pin him to the floor and hold him. His eyes were flashing at me and he started screaming:

"I'll kill you, kill you, I'll do it, damn you. . . !"

But he couldn't get away from the hold I had on him, and finally he just stopped struggling and lay there.

We stayed there like that on the floor for what seemed like a long, long, time. Maybe it wasn't more than just a few minutes. Anyway I finally got up and turned him loose. Papa didn't move for I don't know how long; he just lay there and looked up at me. Then, he said:

"If you stay in here, I'll take your life!"

I looked over to Mama, and she motioned for me to go on outdoors. I did as she asked. And walked on off from the place we lived in then, just walked on to the edge of the woods, feeling pain and anger inside. I didn't know what to do anymore. Nothing came along the way I thought it should, and now here I was fighting with my own father. This was a low feeling, a bad, bad feeling inside me.

I stopped and stood by the road, just lowered my head and said some prayers, tried to speak as plainly and clearly to God as I could. I needed help, and at least I knew that. If I hadn't, well, there's not any telling where my life might have gone from that night. I saw it all over Stockbridge all the time. A man's anger gets the best of him. Violence is the only thing he's got to calm him down some, or get him killed, one day.

I stayed out by those woods most of the night. Mama came

later to tell me that my father was asleep. Still angry, waking up once in a while and groaning about what he'd do when he saw me.

The next day, when he got up, he came walking out on the road where I'd been all night. We stood around for a few minutes, didn't say a word, either of us.

Finally, Papa turned away as he started to talk to me, then turned back to me as he spoke:

"You're all right, boy. But I say to you now, I don't want you goin' up against me like that again, you hear?"

"Yes, sir," I told him.

"All right. And I tell you here and now I won't never hit your Mama again. Y'understand?"

"Yes, sir."

"All right," he said, very quietly, and pushed his hand against my shoulder, just lightly.

And he never hit Mama again. Not ever.

Four

But this incident weighed on my mind. I'd have nightmares about it and wake up shaking in the middle of the night. I really didn't know if the Lord could forgive me, striking out at my father that way. This frightened and confused me. While everybody was sleeping one night, I slipped out of the house and started down the road. There was no plan in my mind, no notion about where I was going or what I'd do when I got there. I felt I had to go. Down in Stockbridge, there was a freight train stopped in the depot. When the engineer climbed back up and started out for Atlanta, I was in one of the boxcars. I just didn't care anymore. Going was all that mattered. Where wasn't important. I leaned back against the side of the car and watched the land rush by as the train picked up speed. I could only hope that Mama would understand and be all right until I could get in touch with her some way or another. And I thought about the other kids, worried about them, but I couldn't turn back. If I didn't go somewhere I was afraid I'd explode.

The next morning I found myself in the Southern Railroad Yards, the section called the Southern Shops, Atlanta, where the train had pulled in for servicing. I jumped down out of the boxcar and wandered around, watching dozens of men, laborers mainly, go about their work. A big man with a badge on his jacket spotted me and came over. "You lookin' for work, nigger?" he asked. I didn't know what to say. Clearly, this fellow took me for a grown man because of my size. All those years of farm work had built me up to where I could easily be mistaken for a person several years older. I put my voice down as low as I could get it and said, "Yessir, I'm lookin' for a job if you got one. . . ." By sunup that morning, I was pushing a broom around the sheds of the Southern Shops of the Southern Railroad, acting just like I belonged, grown up as I could be.

For about a week I slept outside, around the yards or in boxcars when I could find one open. I showed up early for work every day and put in as many hours as the foreman would let me. One night, exhausted, I heard somebody yell out, "Pay call!" and I just followed everybody else over to the foreman. When my turn came he handed me a slip of paper to sign and then handed me twelve dollars in cash. I stood there counting it for the longest time, scarcely believing that it was all mine. But it made me realize, too, just how long I'd been away from home, away from everybody in my family.

"Say, King!" One of the engineers called me aside.

"Yessir," I said.

"Hear tell you can push coal. Ever fired an engine?"

I told him I'd fired cotton gins down in the country, and he said that was good enough. There was a run down to Macon the next day. His regular fireman had a bad arm, burned it when some coals popped out on him from a run during that day. "If you want to earn a little extree money," the engineer said, "you can run on down to Macon with us."

Extree was the term we used for what people call overtime today, and it didn't come easy. Firing coal in a steam engine wasn't just hard, it was very dangerous; men were thrown out of trains moving around turns and killed. But I wanted a shot at that cash, and I knew that having a good reputation around the yards for throwing coal to make steam was just the way to get some. By now I also knew that any success in a place like the yards meant keeping on the good side of the whites when

I wasn't keeping pretty much to myself. I heard the talk, the jealousies and rivalries, talk of how the unions up North were so much stronger and the men were so much better off. I watched men betray each other by reporting on them as union organizers, in a time when organizers weren't welcome in the yards. And I watched as Negroes were passed over for some extree because they'd said something whites thought was said the wrong way, or somebody might not like "some nigger's looks." A lot of learning—about men and work—went into those days I spent working in the yards. I would never feel young again after that, because the thing you don't know when you are young is just how tough all of life really is.

The first few weeks in the yards I slept nights in a toolshed. Nobody asked questions, there were plenty of people and plenty of secrets in railroading. And there were shootings, killings, and brawls going on through the night. To get through, I worked and prayed, and I slept and prayed . . . never once doubted God was working with me.

I threw coal hard and steady. Word got around the yards and the engineers there would offer me a fireman's job whenever a regular man came up sick or missing from work. The money was really good, too, both straight time and the extree, which I often earned by going out at night after my day shift ended. I started dreaming about the time I knew was going to come, when I'd walk into that old cabin back in the country and lay about five hundred dollars out in front of Mama and Papa. The work was rough, at times my whole body just ached, but the thought of seeing my folks smile with the knowledge that something *good* had happened for a change—well, I think I'd have pushed through a pair of brick walls for that. One thing was always clear. I earned every dollar on those fireman runs, and not just because of the work. The hollering of those engineers often hurt more than the sore muscles I dragged into my little pallet in the toolshed when my chance came to get some sleep.

"Nigger!" these trainmen loved to shout. "Come on, nigger, you ain't through yet. Come on, boy, toss that damn coal!"

And of course all I could do was smile the smallest smile I figured I could get away with and go right on pushing. Pretty soon they thought of me as a young bull who could make steam and be a good nigger, too. I thought about the money, and I let them think whatever they wanted to.

Taking the run down to Macon, the train would pass within a hundred yards or so of a hill crest where my brothers and I had played for years. Going through there, I stopped flinging my coal, and got the engineer to let me pull on the train whistle, and I'd give a little signal we all knew. *Toot toot . . . Toot ta toot toot . . . Toot toot.*

And sure enough, one evening, as the run was taking me back to Atlanta, I looked out near the hill crest, and James, Jr., and Henry were running toward the tracks for all they were worth. And I started pulling on the whistle as they waved a red cloth back and forth in front of them. They got close enough for me to see those big grins on their faces, and I just started to cry. The tears were in my eyes all the way back to the yards. I kept telling the engineer there was some coal dust that wouldn't stop flying up into my face.

"But I'm all right, sir," I told him. "I'm just fine."

About a week later, I paid no real attention when the train stopped in Stockbridge on our way back to Atlanta, but when we reached the yards again, I found out that my mother had gotten on board out there in the country. She marched straight into the yard boss's office and shouted: "You got no business workin' a child like this, he's just a boy!"

She gave the boss my true age—fourteen. A few fellows had asked me, and I'd gotten used to saying I was twenty. Nobody had ever doubted me. Well, Bailey, the yard boss, said Mama was right, I *was* too young to be working there, and he'd have to fire me. This just cut right through me. I felt I'd been doing so well. True, I was tired a lot of the time, didn't always eat right, but, hell, I was out in the world earning a living.

Mama looked at me, furious at what I'd done, the worry I'd caused her all these weeks. Bailey told her I had a pretty fair piece of money coming on what I had already done and Mama, flaring up again, told him No! Her boy wasn't taking any more money from this place!

Then she marched me out of the office as Bailey followed,

asking her over and over, "What should I do with his money that he's got comin'?"

"Do what you must with it," Mama shouted back, "but we don't want it!"

And with that she pulled me out of his office. She had me walking in front of her like a little boy, and I could hear men all through the yards snickering at big ol' Mike King, young bull of the railroad, whose Mama had come to see he got home safely. I was nothing but a kid to them now, trying to be a man.

Nothing my mother had ever done hurt me the way this did. And of course there was nothing I could say or do about the way I felt, because it was Mama, and I'd been raised to respect anything she said to me or asked me to do. As a son I couldn't question her on anything. So I tried to explain that there was five hundred dollars back there that I earned, money that was for our family, to give us a few things we hadn't been able to buy before, some dresses for the girls.

"The girls don't need clothes that bad," Mama said.

"Some things for you, Mama, I wanted to get you—"

"I don't want anything, Michael," she answered me, "that gonna cause me to let somebody take advantage of a child of mine. Not for any amount of money in the world will I allow that!"

Maybe, deep down inside, I thought Mama was wrong. I could say nothing. I might have been angry, might have wanted to cry just thinking about that money they owed me in the yards, that I'd never be able to get from there now. But I kept my peace, and never talked after that about what had happened in the yards that day.

In addition to preaching, I had to become a trader. Folks in the country couldn't deal in cash very often. They seldom had much of it, and when they did, money was spent very quickly, often on debts to landowners and the people who ran the local stores. When a preacher came some distance to offer services to a group of folks who had no regular pastor, they'd show their appreciation by giving him what they could. One congregation might have a bushel of potatoes. If the preacher was really good, the people might find a horse to let him have, or even better, a cow, which was the most valuable animal known, next to the mule, out among country people. They'd give whatever they could. And for the young preacher who was ready to settle down and raise a family, plenty of attractive young girls would try to help him to make up his mind. Before long, this young fellow might find himself farming right along with someone who was about to become his father-in-law, and pretty soon, with all the hard work and long hours that went into farming, a preacher found he wasn't doing much preaching anymore.

Keeping on the move, I avoided any early entanglements. I'd always be headed off someplace, trading a hog folks had given me in one town for some gasoline in another. Or maybe I'd split up twenty pounds of berries or pecans, keep some and exchange the rest for secondhand shoes or a suit of clothes. I came in contact with hundreds of people this way, and had to remember not to try and trade a fine cow, for instance, right back to the folks who'd given it to me, very proudly, in the first place.

In my life I would always have a good head for figures; business dealing was as much a part of those early years as interpreting the Bible. Oddly enough, I never came into contact with banks during this time. Every transaction of mine was on faith—this for that—and depended on an honest, old-time, country-folks integrity. Nobody cheated anybody and stayed long in a community of Negro church folks. They'd run someone out of a place in a minute. If you told a man you had a good wagon, that's what he could expect to see when you showed up to take care of some business with him. And if the other fellow said he could trade a nice pocket watch for the wagon, you just knew that's what you'd leave the deal with—a very good watch.

But it seemed, somehow, that when money was introduced into things, people changed, and sharply, right before your eyes. So, for the longest time in my young life, I tried to keep money out of business, strange as that may sound today. But as my preaching impressed more people, so did my trading increase, and soon I found myself going often to Atlanta, just to get cash for a carload of vegetables and fruit that would otherwise spoil before I could use them.

I met a young woman in Atlanta, a very warm and friendly person, Bertha Chaney. Her father was a Methodist minister, an educated, very stately man, the Reverend Wilson Chaney. Bertha and I started keeping company after a cousin of hers from Stockbridge introduced us at a church supper.

Bertha had been a very lonely young woman, and I suppose this had a lot to do with her willingness to go against a prevailing tradition of that era. In Negro communities, there was little social life outside the borders established by church affiliation. People married, did business, went to doctors and dentists, all within the structure of their churches. Methodists often looked down on Baptists, whom they considered not as well educated (which, generally speaking, was true), and more emotional than reasoned in their services of worship (a good case could be made for this point of view, also). To Baptists, the Methodist congregations were often stiff, social-climbing pretenders, people who put on airs until they suffocated everybody around them. When Bertha started seeing me, her father reacted angrily. Her mother simply pretended I didn't exist. Bertha herself was old enough, of course, to make her own life. She worked and contributed to her household with the salary she earned in a small Negro insurance company.

Bertha fell in love with me. I felt extremely unhappy about this, because my feelings for her were not so intense. She was a wonderful companion, cheerful and affectionate, very serious about things like loyalty and truth . . . and, perhaps more than anything else, family. She wanted to marry and have children, which was something a woman in those days could never speak about much, except to very close women friends or relatives. Around men this sentiment was always held in check until, I guess, many women were ready to explode.

Bertha taught me how to use the bank. I carried cash around with me, just stuffed into pockets wherever there was room. Bertha helped me open an account for savings, took me into a world of little cages and books with entries and withdrawals, a world that had been all around me in my life when I didn't even know it. At first I didn't have the confidence to go to the bank by myself. All that writing, counting, double-checking. So, I'd catch a late train into Atlanta on a Thursday night, meet Bertha at the station, and just give her the money I was putting in my account. There was no question of trust, we both knew that, and it made our relationship a very strong one in its own way. And both of us also knew that she wanted more. Trust was a solid ground to build on. And sometimes, on the train ride, I would wonder why I didn't *love* her, in the sense that she was using the term in expressing her feeling for me. I couldn't understand. She was attractive, well-informed, had an earthy, subtle sense of humor. I enjoyed being with her because she went against the grain of what most people said about the Methodists being very rigid, stuffy folks. But my feelings just stopped short of where Bertha wanted them to go. I knew she wanted the words I couldn't offer, not without lying, which I wasn't going to do.

Bertha Chaney's father knew that she was serious about me. Everything he'd done to discourage our relationship failed, and so he resigned himself to what Bertha, at least, hoped was the inevitable. Reverend Chaney began speaking to me with more friendliness in his voice, and I let him do *all* the talking. *No need*, I thought, *for things to get any more complicated than they already are.* One evening in the spring, Bertha and I went to a social at her father's church. This was a kind of Bible class, and afterward there would be some fruit-juice punch in the church basement. To my surprise, Reverend Chaney asked if I would consider offering the sermon at a Methodist retreat that was planned for a coming Saturday. I was taken completely off my guard, and said yes before I gave any real thought to what I was getting into. It turned out to be the most disastrous Saturday I'd ever had. These Methodist folks, first of all, were city people, not transplanted country men and women. My sermon was greeted with a stony silence, and when I reached the point of describing the pain that Jesus suffered carrying his cross to Calvary, my vivid picture caused eyebrows to raise throughout the wooded clearing by a brush arbor, where we'd all gathered to worship God. "Caintcha see him totin' it?" I cried out to the Methodists, who just turned up their noses and fanned themselves a little harder. I preached an extremely short service that day.

Later, Bertha tried to soothe my bruised, embarrassed feelings.

Somehow, though, I couldn't get the picture out of my mind: Reverend Chaney smirking triumphantly as his church choir muffled its laughter. They must have considered me a clown, a comical country bumpkin. Words like "totin'" didn't fit in an Atlanta vocabulary, not among the Methodists, anyway, among those who'd escaped from the country life I was just emerging from. They didn't need any reminders, from preachers or anybody else, of what they'd left behind. I was that kind of reminder, with my dusty, uncreased clothes, my rough country style of speaking, my whole uneducated, green, farmboy personality. I was nothing to them, almost the way I'd been nothing to the white men back in the country, when I'd been just another one of somebody's niggers.

I called on Bertha during the next week, and we sat on her front porch. She cried softly when I said I wouldn't be seeing her anymore, but I knew this was the only way for both of us. My experience with these kinds of partings was limited, and I didn't know when to leave well enough alone. Bertha was hurt, and trying to hang on to her dignity as a person. I said I wanted to be her friend, that anything I ever could do for her I'd be glad to do; all the wrong things a man can say in a situation like that. She turned to me with fury in her eyes and told me to get out and leave her alone.

As I walked down the stairs from the Chaneys' porch, she called out to me: "Oh, Mike King, you've got a lot to learn!"

The words cut into me. I walked a little faster, knowing in my heart that I wanted to run because I knew she was right.

Five

Mama began to sense that I'd be leaving home again. I was eighteen now and it had been more than three years since my adventure with the railroad. But I guess she could see the restlessness coming again, the city-look forming in my eyes. She was concerned because my father, even though I was not helping him much on the farm, was convinced now that he'd kept me down in the country anyhow. That was his victory, small as it was. And he held on to it.

"Just tell him, Michael," said Mama. "Just don't you leave here without sayin' somethin' to your father."

I have never quite understood why this was so difficult. My father and I argued, we had fought, our differences far outweighed the things that made us father and son. Still, I loved him. Not in the demonstrative way some sons can show their fathers, with a lot of attention, a lot of time spent together. That is the way some people can express affection. I knew that James King was a man who wanted more than he could ever have. And what he wanted wasn't really that much—a decent home for his family, a day's pay for a day's work, the freedom to be judged as a human being and not a beast, a nigger, a nightmare in the white mind. But for him, these things were never to happen. *Maybe tomorrow, just maybe*—Papa must have thought that so many, many times. And every time he did, it had to cut through his soul—the fact that, for no reason that could ever make sense, he would not live to see, to feel, to *be* a part of that new day.

When I decided to tell him, he had known, I think, for longer than I had. For weeks he avoided me around the house, turned away when I tried to talk with him out in the yard. Then one morning I trotted out to the far end of our cotton, where he was moving the mule through the new furrows. "Papa!" I called to him. He stopped the mule, but didn't look back at me. I walked around to face him.

"Papa, I got to go on to Atlanta and stay there. . . ."

He wiped his face with a big bandanna he carried in his coverall pockets, and took a long drink from the water jug sitting on a tree stump near his side. He was silent.

"You see, Papa," I told him, "I just wasn't cut out to be here, and I'm sorry for that in some ways. But I got to make the right life for me."

He didn't turn, and when I told him I was going and wouldn't see him for a while, he put down the jug, which he was cradling in his arms, and ginnied up the mule down through the fresh planting ground. I stood and watched him grow smaller and smaller, heading toward the line of woods between the land he worked and the railroad I'd once steamed along, trying to find my way out. It seemed odd. My father was trotting off behind the mule, moving to the edge of the sky; I was not moving at all. Papa was gone, and it was at the moment that he walked away from me that it seemed there was so much to say, so many things we should have talked about. Now, it just never would happen.

I was back in Atlanta to live again. As far as earning myself some money was concerned, I wasn't really worried because I'd never been afraid of hard work. I even thought about trying the yards again, but changed my mind when I thought of how the men there had laughed at me when Mama took me away from my job four years earlier. I found work in a vulcanizing shop, where auto tires were made. After a month, when the boss there turned me down for a raise, even though I turned out more work than anybody in the place, I quit. The same afternoon, I had a job loading bales of cotton. But the pay on that job was even lower than what I'd earned in the tire plant. However, I didn't feel I was being cheated, so I remained there for several months before I found a decent job driving a truck for a business that sold and repaired barber chairs. This job paid fairly well, enough for my rooming-house rent and food.

I'd found a nice place to live and now had a couple of friends who were also planning futures in the ministry. But best of all, Mama went out one day and sold a cow the family had and used the money to buy me a used Model T Ford. It was the most beautiful car in the world as far as I was concerned, and when she had Papa drive her up to Atlanta with it so they could surprise me, I felt I'd never been happier in my life with any present anyone had given me. Nothing, I now felt, could stop me. Nothing.

That Model T came in handy a short time later. Some good old country folks who'd moved to the East Point section of Atlanta asked me to pastor a church they were starting, while I continued my truck-driving job. I went out there and met with them and got a look at the fine wooden building they were putting up and decided, Yes, I'd accept their call to a ministry. Several of the families out in East Point were friends of my mother's from down home, and they'd built up my reputation among the others. I didn't hesitate to preach out there, even though that experience with the Methodists had bothered me for a long time afterward, and certainly didn't help my confidence. But Methodist ministers were formally trained, for the most part. They were college-educated men. My own preaching was rooted in the emotional appeal that country Baptists understood better than anybody in the world; an appeal often led by men, like myself, who were mostly self-trained.

After living in Atlanta for a while, I realized that, to be truly effective, a preacher had to reach people through their minds as well as through their feelings. In this regard I sensed how important Woodie's advice to me about getting an education really was. As I've mentioned, Atlanta didn't have a single high school for Negroes in those days. There was not a library in town that a black person could use. Learning wasn't easy. Sometimes it seemed impossible. When that registrar at the Bryant School told me I'd have to start in fifth grade, I wanted to forget the whole thing.

But finally I buckled down. I studied at the Bryant School for five years. This was a difficult period in my life. I came to realize that much of the capacity for learning I should have developed as a child in the country just never came about. I became bitter, deeply angry about this, blaming Mrs. Low for not teaching us anything. But how hard it must have been for her! To have so many youngsters who knew, early in their lives, that no amount of learning in the world would ever break the ties that held them to the country, held them to the land, as it had held their folks before them. Country life had its own educational system: to know the seasons and the qualities of earth for planting, or being able to face north and feel the colder weather moving down around crops that need a little more time. *These* things made farmers, and most of them couldn't be learned in the schoolhouse. I thought much later, maybe Miz Low understood that, and lived quietly with all the run-down places she had to teach in, without equipment, trying, trying. . . .

I now realized that I had done so well in school back home because I had covered so little ground. And so I came to Atlanta with an educational background so poor that my reading level was barely beyond a rank beginner's. I could hardly write at all, I'd never known there was so much writing to be done. So I was hardly a scholar when I enrolled at Bryant, and I soon was working twice as hard as most other people in my classes just to scrape past.

The English language became so puzzling I thought at first it was some foreign tongue. Words, parts of speech, punctuation, all these things were magic objects to a young country boy sorting out the new puzzle of his life. And so I burned a little midnight oil. Fellows would drop by my room at the boardinghouse and say my eyes were going to fall right out of my head if I didn't stop reading so late at night. I didn't care about that. There was so much before me. Numbers, all sorts of systems, governments, places I never knew existed and would never have heard about without sitting in that school night after night. The grind seemed to get tougher all the time. I had no natural talent for study, and my learning came after long, long hours of going over and over and over the work until I was falling asleep saying my lessons to myself. All this was here, so much to learn.

God is good, I found myself saying, God is good. I'd walk around Atlanta when the summer came and there were warm, sunny days. I'd buy myself a weenie from one of those roasting stands on the street corners, and look up at this city going up around me and I'd say: I'm part of all this, these modern times, when magnificent buildings go up in hardly any time, and cars roar by going maybe thirty miles an hour. Planes flew men in the sky. And I was here, bearing witness. My Lord. . . .

It was at about this time that something happened that would stay in my memory all my life. I was working hard at Bryant School and my constant reading seemed to weaken my vision. One of the guys at school with me suggested I get some glasses. Well, not knowing any better, I went downtown and just walked into the first place I saw with an eye on its sign. This old fellow came running out from behind a curtain to a back room and just stood there staring at me. Suddenly he yelled for me to get out.

"You have no business here!" he shouted, with a very thick accent.

"All I want is some specs, mister," I told him. "Can't you sell me some?"

This threw him. He said he never knew any niggers who needed glasses, none ever came into his place for any. Why did I need them? he wanted to know.

So I told him that I was in school, hoping that an education might help me in the world. He just looked at me. So I told him not to worry about money, I had a job, too, and I'd pay some every week until he had all I owed.

He checked my eyes and told me to come back in a couple of days. When I did, the old fellow just changed part of the world around for me, putting these round metal-rimmed spectacles on me so that I could see, clearly, all there was to see.

"They're yours," he told me. "You take them and study good."

I reached into my pocket for some money. He said no, that was all right, I owed him nothing. He was German, he said, and had come to America right after the World War. "I don't like," he told me, "the way some people are treated, but it is the way things are here, so everyone has to go along. . . ."

"Let me give you some money," I insisted, and as the two of us were standing there at the counter, a white woman walked in with a young girl. They were there to pick up some glasses. The old man looked at them, then turned to me and shouted, "I don't have what you want here, so get out, nigger, before you get in trouble!"

I understood. This old eye doctor knew if the woman saw him doing a favor for a "nigger," heard me thank him for helping me in some special way, she might tell others that he was a nigger-lover or something like that, and he'd find a stone crashing through his window, or a fire eating up his business. I turned and walked out, my ears still ringing from what he'd said, this good old fellow who just wanted to do some little thing that was right, who tried and wasn't able to.

I looked back at him once I was outside, and through the front window of his place I saw that his head was down, as though he was looking through the case where he kept glasses on display, down beyond the floor and the earth itself, looking for a reason why. Well, I've never forgotten him. He was worth remembering.

The principal of Bryant was a man named Charles Clayton, who later became an attorney in Atlanta, not an easy thing to do in those years. He was also my first English teacher, a man of great skill with ability to encourage his students, not only in matters of grammar, but in life as well. So many of the folks at Bryant were convinced from the outset that I would just never make it. Some of them, I now think, might have even admired my tenacity, but not believed at all in my chances to succeed as a student or as anything else. I wanted to prove them wrong, of course, but couldn't do it without help. As a teacher and as principal, Mr. Clayton—who was just a few years older than I when I enrolled at Bryant—made that help available. In between his belaboring many of us about our syntax and abuse of verbs in the English language, he encouraged us to look at a rigidly fixed world and find out where the possibility of change existed. He introduced us to the electoral process and the way in which we, as Negroes, were excluded from it in the South. This, I'd never thought much about. White folks handled all that, I told myself. Who needs to vote? What's there to vote for except one white man or another, both of them trying to keep you back?

Charles Clayton was of a different mind. He urged his students to register as soon as they reached their twenty-first birthdays and were of legal age to vote. Why do this? I wondered. Because, Mr. Clayton pointed out, America isn't a country that stands still. Things change here. Even the South, he went on, will have to change in time. Be ready for tomorrow today. Register because your enemies don't want you to do it, because they know how important it's going to be to vote in the coming years. . . .

Now I was hearing the term *struggle* used to describe what my own life was really about. Negroes were fighting to advance to full citizenship in this country. Playing a role in electoral politics, at whatever level was possible, *could* make a difference. Federal law required that Negroes be offered the opportunity to register and vote in the national elections. The state of Georgia, like the other regions of the South, used methods of intimidation to discourage any effort by blacks to become voters. But even die-hard crackers could be convinced that the might of the federal government wasn't something to be taken lightly. As a citizen of the United States, my right to vote in a Presidential election every four years couldn't be taken away by anybody unless I sat by and let it happen. One night after classes, I caught up with Mr. Clayton in the hallway to make sure I'd understood just what he said on this point.

"That's right," he said. "'You can go right on down to the City Hall and register to vote in the next national election. The crackers may make it rough for you, Young King, but they can't stop you."

So I took him at his word and went down to City Hall. I told a guard I wanted to register, and he looked at me as if I'd just smacked him in the face. But he soon directed me to an elevator

marked COLORED. It wasn't running. A nearby staircase that led
to the registrar's office for COLORED was marked WHITES ONLY.
So a Negro could get to the COLORED registrar's window only by
using the COLORED elevator, which wasn't running. And the
staircase that would have taken a Negro who was willing to
walk up to the office couldn't be used except by whites. I waited
for the elevator half an hour before I gave up in disgust and
left. As I passed by the guard who had given me directions, I
could hear him chuckling at me under his breath. Right then I
decided to come back and keep coming back until the elevator
was running, or until I could find another way to reach the
registration window.

For several days I tried. The white elevator, just a few steps
away, was always running. But I couldn't use that one, of
course. And I'd stand there feeling a rage build up in me as I
watched white schoolteachers herding their young white pupils
onto their elevator so they could tour the Atlanta City Hall
and see just how democracy worked. I don't think any of those
teachers ever took the time to explain to those children why I
was standing there when they rode up and still waiting when
they came back down. Perhaps they never saw me. . . .

But this was only the beginning. Eventually, the elevator
would come, and the Negro waiting for it would be taken to
the Negro registration window. Once there, he'd learn that a
tax was levied on black people who had the uppity nerve to
want some part of a white man's business. These were the
head taxes or poll taxes, as they were called. The Negro who
wished to vote would often have to pay these taxes not only for
himself, but for his ancestors who had resided in the same
county—whether or not these ancestors had ever actually voted
or even been allowed to vote. These taxes could mount up to
such a sum that nobody could pay them. Some Negroes went
back and started saving, then started waiting all over again for
that elevator, and the checking of records at that little window.
Once the money was paid up, if it was, the Negro could then
take a test to determine whether he was educated enough to
vote. (Sometimes he might be eligible to vote under the provisions of the "grandfather clauses," that is, if a direct ancestor
of his had voted during the early Reconstruction days.) Some-

times that would stop him again. The Negro would have to go off and study, get help with all sorts of questions about government and history and the Constitution—which all Negroes really needed to know more about. Maybe that part of it was a strange blessing because some blacks learned a lot about government that way.

There were Negroes who went through it all and eventually came out of City Hall with a card that made them registered voters for the national elections. They came away with something rare and special. Knowing I could vote was one of the most meaningful things in my young life. But if this was any kind of victory over anything, it was just a beginning. The next phase was still years away.

Just before classes one evening, Mr. Clayton called me into his office. My father was there, and he'd been drinking. The work on the farm was going badly. My younger brothers weren't able to help Papa as much as he needed now, so he wanted me back home. I looked at Mr. Clayton, but he stared right back with a look that made it clear I wasn't going to lean on anybody in making this decision. I told my father I couldn't go back, that school was too important, not only to me, but to Woodie Clara. My sister had lost her job when a fire at the yarn factory where she was working closed the place down. So I was picking up her costs and mine, cutting down on the number of classes I was taking so I could earn a little more with overtime. I'd never go back to the farm.

"This is your father you talkin' to, boy," Papa yelled across Mr. Clayton's office. "I say you comin' back an' that's it!"

My throat went dry. All I could remember was that night we'd fought, and how sick it had made me afterward nearly every time I thought about it. Honor thy mother and thy father, the Scriptures told me. But if Papa had grabbed me by the collar, oh, what would I have done? I don't think I could have fought again, that just wasn't in me, not against my father! But I knew also that if it came to that, Papa would drag me back to Stockbridge, just to show he had enough *will* remaining in him to do it.

Suddenly, through all the tension and pressure, I could hear

Mr. Clayton's voice as he spoke gently, persuasively, to my father. "'Don't ask your son to do this, Mr. King," he said. "Not when his future is so clearly tied to his getting an education. We can only give him some of that here, maybe not enough, but let us, and let him try."

"How you payin' for this?" Papa asked me.

"Workin'," I told him. "Doin' odd jobs, drivin' an' such."

"You payin' your way an' ya sister's, too?"

"Tryin' hard, Papa, I'm doin' the best I can."

He stared at me, through all that liquor, through all his days and times. "I need your help, son," he said. "I'm doin' all I can, too, but I can't cut it unless you come on down there an' give me a hand."

The three of us stood silently in that little office, each of us trying to find something, somewhere, to look at besides the floor. "I can't, Papa, I just can't. . . ."

He bit his lip hard, and I saw him lurch toward the door of the office. He turned just as he left, turned and looked back at me, his eyes narrowing, afraid, defiant, angry. He was going back to the country, back to cotton, leaving me, his first son, in a place that made no sense to him at all. For an instant I hated what I was doing. I wanted to run back home and say, Mama, I can't do it, it's too hard, I'm gonna farm just like everybody else.

But I watched my father go and I knew I'd never follow him anywhere again, not down country roads, not through corn or to town or along the railroad tracks back out to where we lived.

I was free, it seemed, in a way I'd dreamed of being, and though I knew it was going to cost me, I was willing to bear the price now, as I watched through Mr. Clayton's window, watched and saw Papa struggle across the street heading down to the bus station and back out to Stockbridge.

I walked back down the hall to my class, which had already started, and I sat down and listened as the teacher went over the lessons we'd been assigned from the previous night. I listened, but I heard very little. . . .

Six

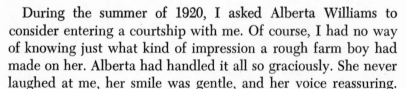

During the summer of 1920, I asked Alberta Williams to consider entering a courtship with me. Of course, I had no way of knowing just what kind of impression a rough farm boy had made on her. Alberta had handled it all so graciously. She never laughed at me, her smile was gentle, and her voice reassuring.

Well, I really didn't know much about falling in love. Maybe nobody ever really does. I'd been sweet on a few girls back in Stockbridge, but never in a way that took hold very seriously. Out there, in those days, a pregnant girl was a married girl, a young man who became a father also became a husband if he intended to stay around those church folks. So most young men, and I'd have to say especially young preachers, had to be pretty careful in their social lives. But with Alberta Williams, I felt something new, and knew that I'd have to see her again . . . and again.

The Williams house on Auburn Avenue was a few blocks away from the Bryant School, and I took to walking past it nearly every evening on my way to and from my classes. I was hoping to see Alberta sitting on her porch, but she was never there; she usually came only for Sunday services at her father's church. The rest of the time she was at Spelman where, except for the Sunday afternoon social gathering in the dormitory parlor, she could not receive visitors or even any messages.

One evening, as I was walking very slowly past the house, her father came out on the porch to take a stretch in the cool evening air. I couldn't make up my mind whether I wanted to keep moving or stop right there in mid-stride. Just when I was getting ready to greet him, the Reverend turned around, without ever seeing me, and went back into his home. But I truly believed that good things would come to those who waited. Finally, my opportunity developed, very casually, one Saturday night. Alberta had been at a wedding her father officiated at in Ebenezer, and decided to stay over for church the next morning. I'd driven down to Stockbridge with Woodie, to see Mama, and was dropping her off at the Williamses', where she was still rooming, when I saw Alberta walking toward the house along Auburn.

She remembered me, although it had been months since we first met. "Oh, I couldn't forget meeting a preacher, my father wouldn't allow it," she said. Woodie excused herself and went into the house, and Alberta and I stayed out on the porch to chat. She seemed to know about everything and talked so freely, with such ease and such style! Finally, she complimented me on the way I kept my car up, very neat and polished, always in good repair.

"Well, let me carry you out for a ride sometime," I said to her. She looked surprised, then she chuckled a little. Her father would never allow that!

"Well, the truth is," I told her, "that I'm preachin' pretty good along in here, and I was wonderin' if you ever thought about courting. I'd like to if you'd consider it."

"Court?" she said. "But I don't know you, Reverend King."

"No better'n I know you," I answered. "Difference is that I'm interested in findin' out more about you, 'cause you seem to me such a fine person, very gracious and all."

This shocked her, I think; nobody had ever asked her to court. And Alberta had set her heart and mind on teaching school. This was her consuming interest—the future of the children in our community.

For a long time she just stared at me. "I . . . I'm not sure what my folks would say," she told me.

I said, "Well, maybe we'd better find out first what you think. Could I come and take you for a drive one time when you're home?"

"That's so very nice," she said. "It's the nicest thing. But I'd have to ask my folks. . . ."

"Well, ask them," I said to her. "I mean, if it's all right with you."

"Why, yes," she said, "I think I'd like that very much!"

And so we started a courtship that lasted six years. This wasn't uncommon in those days. Marriage was regarded with great seriousness, and almost never entered into lightly. Alberta and I went for our drives, and after some real work at convincing Reverend Williams, we went to see a movie being shown in town, back then when they were called picture shows. This was a very happy period in my life. "I think about you a lot, Alberta," I'd often tell her, "about what a fine life two people like us ought to try and have in this world."

One night, her father came out on the porch while Alberta and I were talking. He sent her inside and sat down for some talk, man-to-man, with me. Alberta's education wasn't going to be interrupted, he made it very clear. "We don't have any spare rooms in this house for broken hearts, son."

Well, I knew what he meant and quickly I tried to make him understand that I had nothing but honorable intentions where Alberta was concerned. "In fact," I told him, "I'm hopeful I can convince her to consider marrying me, Reverend Williams."

Alberta was returning with a tray of lemonade just as I started talking about *my* plans for *our* future. She put the lemonade down next to her father, looked at me, and rushed back into the house, where she and her mother soon started taking turns trying to calm each other down. Reverend Williams said he couldn't hear himself think for the sound of their voices, and *he* went inside to try and quiet them down. Then I heard Woodie's voice, and one of the elderly sisters who was boarding with the Williams family at the time, and soon it sounded like a choir rehearsing in there.

Woodie suddenly reappeared on the front porch. We held hands and stood there looking at each other, starting to say things and not finishing the sentences, as the voices from inside grew louder and happier.

A few minutes later it was still going on. A few neighbors had come by, and Mrs. Williams was serving lemonade. The Reverend and I took a walk down Auburn, along the way where Negro businesses were springing up and flourishing as a new Atlanta started to grow. Reverend Williams spoke of the new city and of the days ahead for it. The black population was not only large but many in it now owned property and were sending record numbers of children to college.

"It's goin' to be different here in a few years, King," the Reverend said. "Change is comin' whether the white man can handle it or not. There may be a lot of difficult times, and I hope you're a man ready to deal with it. But let me be clear about something. This isn't the time for you and Alberta to be thinking about gettin' married. She's got school to finish, and you've got your ministry to establish."

I told him I could respect that view, but that Alberta and I had been very attracted to each other from the first day we ever met. "It's not gonna change, sir," I told Reverend Williams as we walked back toward his home.

And so our courtship blossomed, and I was soon known in the congregation of Ebenezer as Alberta's preacher beau. My life blossomed, too. I had my little Model T Ford, and I'd take a drive with Alberta nearly every weekend. Or we'd convince Reverend Williams, over and over, that these moving-picture shows folks were running didn't have so much sin in them that good Baptist people couldn't enjoy attending. Church folks then didn't drink or smoke or dance with each other. I had grown up that way in the country, just as Alberta had in the city. Social life was built completely into the framework of the church. But it wasn't as rigid as many people say. There were picnics and boatings and drives, plenty of good food among very warm, affectionate people.

Everything was strictly chaperoned, of course, even the teas they held at Ebenezer, where nobody would dare get out of hand anyway, even if none of the older members were around.

Usually, the older saints of church did the chaperoning, women who'd raised children and spent all their years praising the Lord in the hardest of times. Negro people had a closeness and sense of family that made for very strong bonds of emotional security. I was very happy.

But the next fall Alberta left Atlanta to study at Hampton Institute, in Virginia. I was just torn up inside when she told me. But her parents felt we needed some time apart to let our senses cool off some. We'd both told them we were in love that summer. Marriage was the next step. But there was one hitch. The board of education in Atlanta had a rule against hiring women to teach if they were married. Reverend and Mrs. Williams had grown very fond of me in a very short time. But they weren't about to sacrifice their daughter's education and training before she had any chance at all to use it. They frankly wanted us to test this love we talked about so much and so happily. So Alberta went away to Hampton and studied there for nearly a year and a half. Our only communication during this time was by letter. But our affection for one another simply found another way of expressing itself.

When Alberta came home for good, after finishing her courses up at Hampton, I drove down to the railroad station and stood in the door of the colored waiting room on this very rainy afternoon and then ran along the platform when I saw her and just swept her up into my arms.

"Aw, there you are," I shouted. "My little bunch of goodness is back with me again! I love you, just love you more than anything in this world."

She was laughing. "What's this bunch-of-goodness business?"

"Well," I said, "that's what you are to me. But I'll shorten it up some if you want and just call you Bunch!"

Bunch and I had our engagement announced by her father during Sunday morning services at Ebenezer, and as we stood outside afterward, greeting people, accepting congratulations, I began to notice that many of the church folks seemed to take it for granted that I was now going to be Reverend Williams's associate pastor.

* * *

It was the greatest period of happiness I'd ever known. But it was interrupted in 1924. One afternoon in the spring, I drove over to the bus depot to meet my brothers Henry and James, Jr., who were coming up from Stockbridge for a weekend in the city. From the moment they got off the bus, I knew something was wrong. Mama, they finally told me, was doing very poorly in her health, but didn't want me to worry.

"But it's real bad, Mike," they told me, and I could see both of them had been crying. So we just turned around and drove down to Stockbridge, with my thoughts and feelings turning over even faster than the wheels of the car. My blood just rushed at the thought of anything being wrong with my mother, and when we arrived and I saw her, I knew my very worst fears were accurate.

A huge tumor had developed on her neck, just below her chin. She had so much pain she couldn't turn her head, and this tumor had been growing there for months. The boys told me some old country doctor had sold Mama some medicine that made her even worse, it seemed to them. Now I was angry and felt like going out and grabbing that old quack and shaking the life out of him. But Mama was so happy to see me. And I realized I'd been planning to do so much for her that I no longer visited regularly. I was ashamed of that, and told her I'd do much better from now on.

Mama just smiled and shook her head. "It's all right, son."

Later that evening, when she fell asleep, I jumped back into my car and drove on up to Atlanta. One of my boardinghouse mates had a cousin who was a doctor there in town, and this young man agreed to come back down to Stockbridge with me and take a look at Mama. I prayed to myself all the way there, running much too fast over those country roads, but, of course, not concerned about driving safely.

Back in Stockbridge, the doctor examined the swelling on Mama's neck, then walked with me along the road outside the cabin.

"It's very bad, Mike. There's really nothing that can be done for her now," he told me. "Just keep her as comfortable as you can."

"How long?" I asked him.

"A few months . . ."

I dropped out of school and went down to Stockbridge to spend my mother's last days with her. She was in agony most of the time now; no matter what medicine she took, nothing helped very much. She took comfort in my reciting Scriptures to her, and I concentrated on the Psalms, which she loved hearing, until, one morning, she passed into a deep sleep and began to breathe heavily and to moan. That noon, she died.

We buried her several miles away, near the school I'd attended, which was near the church of Reverend Low, the husband of our teacher. Papa was just ruined by Mama's death. She'd suffered so much, and he'd been able to do nothing, offer no comfort. It cut into him. He took it hard and thought that whiskey would help. His grief just broke him down at the graveside, and none of us could do anything to help. And in the sound of his pain I heard Papa's love for Mama, and I heard the years they'd spent trying to build a life in a place where the Negro wasn't regarded as a human being.

During those final nights, when she was slipping away from us, I cursed the whites who took so much away and inflicted so much hatred and violence on people whose color they didn't happen to share. I told Mama, as I had years ago, that I'd hate every white face I ever saw, but she made me promise I'd never let that happen. "Hatred," she told me, "makes nothin' but more hatred, Michael. Don't you do it."

But as I looked at my father that day we buried Mama, and saw so many of the scars that had been left on my parents, I really didn't know how I could keep that promise.

I grieved deeply for many weeks afterward. And several months after Mama's death, the family suffered another tragedy when my sister Ruby suffered from a ruptured appendix and died suddenly. All this grief brought home very clearly that running away from the country had solved very little for me. The pressure of discrimination and bigotry followed very closely, country or city, wherever people's skin was dark. White supremacy took different forms in Atlanta, but it was always around, just as it had been back there in the country. Whites had invented the "nigger," who lived everywhere and suffered wherever he lived. And when the nigger was finished hauling water and wood, he could always serve as somebody to be blamed for what was wrong anywhere. Southern politicians built up whole careers with a single issue: Niggers. Not people. Niggers. Not life. Niggers. Whites became twisted out of shape when it came to race. Some hated very quietly, just going along instead of actually doing any of the hating themselves. Southerners developed looking-the-other-way into an art. Seeing no evil, they could feel certain they were responsible for none. But it was there—in the lynch mobs that ran free in the rural areas, in signs all over Atlanta that separated human beings by color and channeled their lives through doors that read WHITES ONLY or COLORED ENTRANCE.

People were like zombies within the system of southern segregation. Whites often apologized for it, but none of them ever moved on their own to do anything about ending the lie of separate but equal lives for the races.

Alberta, whom I now called Bunch all the time, urged me to involve myself even more in my studies. Finishing Bryant was fine, she felt, but it should not be the end of my formal education. Reverend Williams had attended Morehouse College for a year, and he advised me to look into taking some courses over there. And so, in the fall of 1926, I walked into the Morehouse registrar's office and told the young man there, a fellow named Lloyd O. Lewis, that I was ready to start college. He was skeptical, and he had reason to be. Mr. Lewis gave me some tests. He was a very able and demanding fellow, and after he'd marked my exams he said, bluntly, "You're just not college material, Reverend King."

I was furious. It seemed that folks kept telling me I couldn't do things that I then went out and did.

"I can handle anything you've got here," I told Mr. Lewis. "If hard work'll git it, I ain't got a problem."

But in Lewis's opinion, college required more than hard work. A student had to have a background, something to build on, a foundation. According to Lewis, I didn't have that. "Nothing personal," he assured me.

I left his office thinking I should have been satisfied with my diploma from Bryant, but realizing that this would never be enough when there was so much more to learn. Bunch put it all in perspective. "You're not an educated man, King, not yet. You've got work to do, and you've got to get started."

But to return to school at my age seemed more than just difficult. So I had almost convinced myself, after that initial effort to enroll at Morehouse, that scholarly pursuits just weren't going to be part of my life anymore; but Bunch wasn't impressed by my viewpoint on this matter. She convinced me that I had to continue my studies.

Unfortunately, Lloyd Lewis, too, was unmoved. When I visited his office again, he stuck to his original judgment that I'd be wasting my time and the college's if I tried to pursue a course of study at Morehouse. I asked if he'd give me a trial, a term, say, to prove I could do the work. He listened patiently, but still concluded that I *couldn't* do the required work, and my test scores were all the evidence he needed to decide.

I left his office feeling as if I'd been kicked. My spirit was torn, and I just walked around the school for nearly an hour. Then I made a decision, a very reckless one. I walked back into the Morehouse Administration Building, straight past the secretary and into the office of the president of the college. Once inside, I stopped cold.

President John Hope was clearly not a man you just walked in on. He glared at me from the other side of his large, ornate desk, with eyes that seemed to burn right through mine. But I looked him straight back in the eye and said, "Sir, my name is Mike King, Reverend Mike King, and I know, sir, that my tests are not too good. But I want to go on in school, I want more education, and if there's any way I can come here to Morehouse . . ."

He stood up, and I thought about sinking right through the floor. When I told him that I failed all the tests Mr. Lewis had given me, his eyes hardened even more. "But, sir," I said, "when I came to Atlanta I couldn't even read, I had to go to grammar school to learn anything. And I put in five years, I know a lot more than I did! I can go further, if I work at it, and I will."

When I'd poured all this out, President Hope seemed so unimpressed that I turned to leave. I'd reached the steps of the

Administration Building when the secretary caught up with me and said that the president wanted me back in his office. I ran there, tried to calm myself down, and went in again. He stared at me, said nothing, then handed me an envelope with the registrar's name on it and waved me out of his office. Quickly, I returned to Mr. Lewis's office and gave him the letter. As he read it, the expression on his face changed from amusement to anger.

"Apparently," he snapped, "you can begin classes at Morehouse. Don't ask why, but you can. . . ."

My old mates at the boardinghouse gradually scattered to the winds, moving to different parts of Atlanta or to other places in the United States. At Morehouse I had little time for the ordinary framework of social life. I was older than most students, engaged to be married, and already practicing my profession as a preacher. And so I made only one good friend while I was there, a young student minister from Texas. Sandy Ray was his name, and we were to be friends for many years after our student days. We shared an awe of city life, of cars, of the mysteries of college scholarship, and, most of all, of our callings to the ministry. Like good pals should, we tried to help each other with studies. It didn't take either of us long to realize that that wasn't going to work too well; both of us needed better assistance than that. I was fortunate to have a fiancée recently out of college herself, who could explain, as patiently as possible, what was the obvious to her. What I learned I passed along quickly to my friend Sandy, before it became mysterious all over again.

Where Sandy and I were really able to reinforce each other, though, was in the common view of religious life both of us had as kids and had carried into our adulthood. Sandy viewed the opportunity to provide moral leadership and Biblical commitment to a congregation as the most challenging task he'd ever known. He knew, as I did, that some of those old country preachers back home in Texas and in Georgia used the church for gain, for one kind of profit or another. This gave the Negro Baptist minister a reputation, among some folks, as a confidence man who took advantage of the poor and the ignorant. Yet even from their bad example, Sandy would say, we can learn how the road *should* run, and make our way along a better path.

But Sandy wanted another kind of environment than the South for his work, while I was committed to stay in that part of the country. He was convinced I could put together a great pastorate in one of the northern cities with a sizable population of transplanted Georgians.

"Think about a place like Cincinnati," Sandy'd tell me. Well, I'd been there and swore I wouldn't go back. My sister Woodie had made an unfortunate marriage to a preacher from there, a man who said he was a preacher, anyway. I'd made the mistake of accepting an invitation from him to attend a revival he organized. But this fellow was just a trifler, and I took a train all the way to Cincinnati just to find that out. So few attended that the revival turned into a shambles. And I soon discovered that Woodie, who had left a very fine teaching opportunity behind in Atlanta when she fell in love with this man, was living a wretched life. She was doing whatever seamstress work she could, because her husband really didn't know how to make a dime. I gave her all the money I had in my pocket when I left and told her to review very carefully in her mind what the alternatives were to this kind of an existence. Soon afterward I was happy to hear that she'd left the man when he started to become abusive. Eventually she remarried happily and moved to the city of Detroit.

This episode had left a bad taste in my mouth, not just for Cincinnati but for the whole myth of northern opportunity. Up there I saw for the first time that streets weren't paved with gold as I'd thought they were when, as a child, I visited some of our relatives in Ohio. They had shown me the better-looking houses and shopping areas and had made the North into a rosy picture for a wide-eyed country boy. Now I could see things clearly—I had a better view, a more honest look at what was real.

"Nothin' up North I've lost," I told Sandy. "I'm a part of Georgia. I know my way around here."

As it turned out, Sandy's first call to a pastorate was at

LaGrange, Georgia. He did get out of the "down home" area after that, however, going to churches in Chicago and in Columbus, Ohio, after serving at two more in Macon, Georgia. His major call, though, the one that anchored his career as a minister, was at the famed Cornerstone Baptist Church, in Brooklyn, New York, where he distinguished himself in the pulpit for more than forty years.

Seven

Bunch and I were married on Thanksgiving Day, November 25, 1926, in the sanctuary of Ebenezer Baptist Church, by the Reverends James M. Nabrit, Peter James Bryant, and E. R. Carter. It was one of the grandest occasions of my life, seeing my family gathered with me along with Bunch and her folks, and several of my old mates from the boardinghouse who only showed up, I think, to blink their eyes in disbelief. I was just a little nervous during the ceremony, sensing that something, or someone, was missing. When I discovered that Sandy Ray wasn't there, I was furious with him. Later, though, I found out that as much as he'd wanted to come, he stayed away because he had no clothes he considered good enough to wear to his good friend's wedding. He hadn't wanted to embarrass us by coming to the church in any patched-up outfit, so Sandy stayed home. It hurt me when I found out. So much of what we were seemed to come back again and again to how much money we had. And I began thinking, that very day of my wedding, that I should consider again whether to stay in the ministry or go on out into the business world, where I just knew there was a fortune waiting to be made!

But everyone was making a fuss over my being Reverend Williams's son-in-law. Even though I was preaching at two churches at the time, folks who knew the Reverend A. D. Williams were certain he had plans for me as his associate pastor at Ebenezer.

But I resisted this, not wanting any suspicion that I was only after a new pulpit when I married Alberta Williams. In Baptist circles, family was extremely important. At conventions and revivals, a lot of conversations had to do with pastorates and marriages, the joining of congregations and families that had businesses or professions. I wanted no whispers about the reasons Alberta and I were first engaged and then married. I knew my heart, she knew hers. Our love was very deep, but rumors could bring a lot of distress into the strongest homes. I decided to stay with my own congregations, even after Reverend Williams made it clear that he'd be overjoyed to have me with him at Ebenezer. He was, after all, getting on in years, and a good, solid church like Ebenezer Baptist, he said, wasn't a place to leave in the hands of someone who was not capable of handling such a responsibility.

Well, it pleased me no end to realize he had that sort of confidence in me. But I held back. Bunch loved her father, and she had the closest ties to his church. Gently, quietly, she would sometimes urge me to reconsider. I'd smile and say the folks at Ebenezer had an outstanding leader in Reverend Williams. They were in good shape. But out in East Point and College Park, people respected and needed my ministry. I had to stay with them.

We moved into the upstairs portion of the Williams home on Auburn Street and began our life together. What some people now call the extended family was very much a part of Negro life in those days, and Reverend and Mrs. Williams had always kept their home filled with aunts, cousins, friends of the family, boarders—anyone who required a place to live in solid Christian harmony.

In many ways it was an entirely new life for me. Bunch's mother made me feel completely welcome there, however. I was a son to her—though not immediately, because both she and Reverend Williams had always maintained reservations about Bunch's marrying and possibly abandoning her career in education. For his part, the Reverend kept a close eye on me, not just because I was now family, but also because of his deep interest in the direction of the ministries of younger men in Atlanta. It was through him that I came to understand the larger implications involved in any churchman's responsibility to the community he served. Church wasn't simply Sunday morning and a few evenings during the week. It was more than a full-time job. In the act of faith, every minister became an advocate for justice. In the South, this meant an active involvement in changing the social order all around us.

Reverend Williams made it clear to me from the time I moved into his home that he felt no sympathy for those who saw no mission in their lives, who could not understand, for instance, that progress never came without challenge, without danger and, at times, great trial. These obstacles, however, could not stop the true man of God. A minister, in his calling, chose to lead the people of his church not only in the spiritual sense, but also in the practical world in which they found themselves struggling.

Nobody could ignore the political framework that touched every life, Negro or white, in every state of the South in this period. There were blacks, of course, who settled comfortably into the pattern of segregation. And there were ministers who accepted the role of keeping peace between the races at any cost, which usually meant keeping Negroes calm in a crisis, or just keeping them out of touch with the way the rest of the world was moving.

And it is clear, to this day, why this attitude often prevailed. As the one black person in the southern communities of that era who could command any respect whatever from whites for himself and those he might represent, the clergyman was extremely cautious in his dealings with whites. Losing that privileged status was something few clergymen were prepared to risk. Instead of championing the rights of their members, a lot of these ministers simply took their orders from whites and passed them along to Negroes. And the message was simply one of accommodation and silence in the face of segregation's brutal treatment of the Negro. Some church leaders never rocked the boat. They went along with the white establishment's program, whatever it was, and were grateful for whatever little crumbs might spill off the white man's table.

That was not Reverend Williams's way, and neither would it be mine.

In September of 1927, our first child was born, and we named her Willie Christine. But our joy was tempered by a crisis. The little baby fell ill almost right away. A high fever rose in her and refused to subside. The doctors who came could do nothing, and so little Willie Christine suffered great pain and distress. She would cry so, and for such a long time, that in the night I would often put on a robe and go down to walk back and forth on the front porch, looking along Auburn Avenue but not really seeing it. The severity of this illness gave deep concern to both Bunch and me, although, along with her parents, I tried to keep as much worry from her as possible. Bunch was in a very weakened condition after giving birth. She knew, of course, that the baby was not doing well, and this placed some strain on her recovery. I prayed for the Lord's help and wisdom, realizing again, as I had when my mother passed, that His are the final decisions; we will always go along with them.

For nearly two weeks the baby cried almost around the clock, often shaking violently. Finally, late one night, the crying stopped. I was downstairs on the porch by myself, and when I didn't hear her anymore I rushed into the house and found her, wide-eyed and at ease in her body. I just stared. Like that, it was over, just stopped. And soon she was growing, like all babies, crying mostly when she was hungry, giving Bunch and me the happiness that is only for those who deeply love children.

Now, sometimes when I recall those frightening first days of Christine's life, I feel that the illness, as severe as it was, may have strengthened her for the inordinately heavy responsibilities which would become a daily part of her adult years.

There was increasing pressure now to join Reverend Williams at Ebenezer. We were close as a family, and both Bunch and her mother took very active roles in the life at the church. It seemed peculiar, to all of us, that only I wasn't involved there. But Reverend Williams was a very clever man. After supper, he and I would always find ourselves sitting in the parlor talking, whether or not this was what I'd planned.

"How're you doin', Young King?" he'd ask. "How are those churches of yours comin' along?"

Under his very clear direction, the conversation would go to the way in which churches had to be run as they became larger. Community service then became a priority. Youth activities. The organization and training of choirs and secretaries and church boards of various kinds. Money must be carefully handled. Visits to the sick and shut-in, the elderly. All these things had to be *organized*, he stressed. And I'd listen, because all the while he told me these things, there would be times when he'd digress and talk about himself in little spurts, before remembering that he was supposed to be lecturing a reluctant pupil.

A man of firm determination, strong self-reliance, and broad vision, Reverend Williams came to Atlanta on his thirtieth birthday from Greene County, Georgia, where he had been a "country preacher." He inherited his gifts, he said, from his father, who had been a slave exhorter. Intrepid and enterprising, after he arrived in Atlanta he worked in a machine shop and pastored a small church in nearby Kennesaw, Georgia.

In 1894, Ebenezer Baptist Church, then a young, struggling institution in its eighth year, called Reverend Williams to its pastorate, where he remained the pastor until his sudden death in 1931. Under his leadership, the church became a forceful influence in the Negro community, and in the community at large, as I relate later in this chapter.

From the little boxlike structure where Reverend Williams began with the Ebenezer membership, to the church which they built near Auburn Avenue, to two other locations, Reverend Williams led the membership to Auburn Avenue and Jackson Street, where construction for the present building was begun in 1914 and completed in 1922.

Reverend Williams cut quite a figure. He was a tall man, with a frame straight as a steel rod and a complexion like oak.

He was a great speaker, but he often had his troubles with the language. In the pulpit he was very impressive because of his powerful, thundering style. He was a very *involved* person, and in those early years, while I was still a boy out on the farm, Reverend Williams experienced the terrible racial violence that took place in Atlanta during the year 1906, when several Negroes were killed and many more were attacked and injured by the police. The causes of this outbreak were never entirely clear, but the South and especially Atlanta were shaken by it. In an effort to prevent any repetition, a number of Negro ministers formed an alliance that eventually was called the Atlanta Civic League, an advisory board that met with city officials to curb any racial conflict in the city.

But like many churchmen of his time, Reverend Williams was drawn to membership in a small but growing organization called the National Association for the Advancement of Colored People, one of whose founders, W.E.B. Du Bois, was a member of the faculty of the prestigious Atlanta University. For Reverend Williams, the cause of freedom burned deeply inside. The South had created the monster of segregation with enormous care and refused to consider other ways of life. If the spirit could abide it, life might simply settle quietly into a system where humiliation and danger were constant. Some folks learned to live with it, smiling or sometimes just never changing their expressions, every day going deeper into a world of futility and hopelessness, and going without a murmur. But others opposed this southern convention whenever and however they could. Throughout Atlanta, during those early years of the twentieth century, meetings took place that shaped the period that the United States would know half a century later as the Civil Rights Era. Those earlier years were not so dramatic, and the actions that resulted were never quite so prominent. But in the Negro churches, during the long hours of night, folks argued and planned and moved and persuaded others to join them. It was here that what became the South's most effective weapon in later struggles may well have been born. In the years just after 1906, it became popular to characterize Negroes in very derogatory terms in the press.

One Atlanta paper, *The Georgian*, went to great lengths to be insulting when people of color were described in its stories. In a bold move, Reverend Williams went one day to the offices of this newspaper and asked to see the publisher. The publisher was so startled that a Negro would be crazy enough to walk into a white man's office for any reason other than cleaning the floor that he came out and talked. Of course, when the reverend told him why he was there, this fellow ordered him off the premises, yelling that no nigger was going to dictate editorial policy for white folks, not ever!

Reverend Williams moved quickly after that exchange, and within hours brought several churchmen together at Ebenezer. They came up with an idea and set it in motion. A lot of the advertising in *The Georgian* came from stores and other businesses patronized by blacks. The following Sunday, Reverend Williams and his fellow ministers added to their sermons an appeal that these businesses be avoided. In a few weeks, several hundred Negroes around Atlanta were altering their buying habits. They were very private about this, however, not talking about it in public, but just going about the task of protecting their own interests. Well, it didn't take the local shopkeepers and store owners long to see what was going on, and it didn't take them too much longer to notice the connection between *The Georgian*'s use of epithets when describing Negroes and the drop in their profits when these same Negroes looked at the paper's ad pages.

But, of course, a boycott is very tricky business. Folks participating in one had to be extremely cautious; their jobs, even their safety, could be put right on the line with such an action. A lot of pressure can be applied, and some folks will not act honorably. The history of the South is filled with betrayals of one kind or another. Reverend Williams was never turned away from his vision of a better day for his people, but he did see other efforts, other boycotts, come apart because of the factions that were formed, the jealousies, the competitive elements that scattered many movements before they could get off the ground. But the action against *The Georgian* worked. The paper collapsed financially several months later, bitterly denouncing the nigger troublemakers who were taking over

Atlanta, and hinting that there were still some white folks left who knew how to handle them.

Through these years, the ways of southern whites became even more clear to me as I realized how complex the issue of race really was. Some whites claimed to want things changed, but not enough to work at it. Few realized how imprisoned they also were in a system that made *them* obey a set of laws only fools could take seriously. Whites, rich or poor, were chained to segregation as an ethic, bound up with it so tight they could scarcely breathe sometimes. But no one emerged from among the whites of the South who was strong enough to come out and say that this primitive design for living had to end. No one came from among them. It could have ended sooner, far sooner, if someone had.

My studies at Morehouse were the toughest of my life. In the beginning I often seemed at a total loss when trying to grasp dozens of concepts in language, mathematics, and the sciences that some of my teachers felt I should have mastered years earlier. And at Morehouse there were no acceptable excuses. Everybody there was expected to achieve. Faculty members like Miss Constance Crocker, who taught freshman English, were proud of their skills as educators and had no patience with slow learners. She failed me in her course during my first term at Morehouse, flunked me again when I took it over in the second term, then finally gave me a *D* when I took it a third time in summer school.

I couldn't quit because there were always so many other students there reminding each other every day that Morehouse men didn't do that, Morehouse men didn't quit. And so I stayed and flunked courses, took them over, passed them the second time around. Only in freshman English, Constance Crocker's course, did I have to take something more than twice to pass it. She later became the wife of James Nabrit, the minister who had married Bunch and me. They'd all kid me about it years later as we grew to be good friends with the Nabrits.

Two more children were born while I was still in school: Mike, Jr., on January 15, 1929, and Alfred Daniel on July 30, 1930. I was still known as Mike King at this time, although my father insisted until the day he died, in 1933, that he had named me the day I was born and my name was Martin, for one of his brothers, and Luther, for another one.

I'd never had a birth certificate. They weren't common around the turn of the century in places like Stockbridge, Georgia. During his last hours, Papa asked me to make my name officially what he said it was. When he was dying, we spent some hours together talking in his room at the house he and my brothers and sisters had moved to in Atlanta. He had tried so hard to change. He quit drinking, came to church, and seemed to make peace with himself and with his God. When he was gone I took out the necessary legal papers and was therefore called Martin Luther King, Sr. And little Mike became M.L. to his family, although his friends were still calling him Mike many years later. Alfred was always A.D. to us all.

The boys came along as the Depression was hitting America. In addition, both births were extremely difficult for Bunch; but she was convinced there would be great joy for us in a large family. I worried, though, about her physical well-being. Pregnancy had proven very painful to her, birth had left her in an ill and weakened condition. But later several doctors assured Bunch there was absolutely no reason for her not to have more children, as many as she felt she wanted. And Bunch and I were two of the happiest people in all the world.

Just a few weeks before A.D. was born, I completed my studies at Morehouse and received a bachelor's degree in theology. And though I'd never become an outstanding student in college, my stubborn determination got me through. I'd gone to summer school to improve grades and to take make-up courses. Several times I studied myself into complete exhaustion and wanted, so many times, just to stop and never open a book or go to another class again in my life. And when I did graduate, I was ten years older than most of my classmates, but that no longer mattered, though it did bother me at times during my stay at Morehouse.

Graduation proved to be a thrilling experience. Receiving my degree was the final mark in a test of my personal will. The late nights of cramming for examinations, the extra work and the tutoring I'd received pushed me to limits I wasn't always certain I could endure. But so many people had believed in me. When I was weary and down in spirit, Bunch would simply remind me of how far I'd already come—too far to stop along a road where there simply was no turning back. I could not "un-educate" myself, Bunch would point out, so I needed to think only about going on until the job was done. She spoke often about the feeling of accomplishment that came when a lot of very hard work had been completed. There had been times during those four years at Morehouse when I was willing to forgo the feeling. But on that summer day in 1930 when I was graduated, so many of my thoughts centered on just how far beyond our self-imposed limits we can actually go.

Times were tough for everybody as the Depression swept into Atlanta in the early Thirties. Church memberships fell off sharply in some parts of the city. A mood of great fear and disillusionment took hold of many people. I was then pastoring at the small church in the East Point section. The members had very little money, and to make ends meet for Bunch, the children, and myself, I assumed the pulpit of Traveler's Rest Baptist Church as well. When things grew worse for my congregations, they'd do like good country people do and bring food to services to share with the preacher. My family always ate well.

Reverend Williams considered our fairly good fortune part of a call to very special duty. This was the Lord's call. He said to endure and have faith. Whosoever carries the word must make the word flesh. Reverend Williams told the Ebenezer family one Sunday morning that to say is one thing, to live is another. People must be helped in this bitter season.

Ebenezer became a church where the service lasted around the clock. Membership had held at a steady two hundred people. They were a generous congregation, and what money Reverend Williams could take in he poured back into the community to make food available to the hungry and clothes to those without them. We kept children while mothers worked. The church bought and supplied medicines. Ebenezer tried to be an anchor as the storm rose. And we did well—nothing fancy, no frills. But the church helped as many in need as the church could reach. And the church grew stronger.

At this critical time in the spring of 1931, the family suffered a severe blow when Reverend Williams passed away. As he played one morning with granddaughter Christine in the living room of our home, he was stricken with a heart attack. Christine was then three years old and didn't really understand what had happened to her grandfather. She got up and went into the kitchen where her mother and grandmother were preparing breakfast and said that her grandfather was lying on the floor asleep.

The Reverend's funeral was a huge and emotional ceremony. Bunch and her mother took his death in great sorrow. I'd lost a mentor, the good man and fine preacher who'd been friend and father-in-law for enough time for me to miss him a great deal when he'd gone on home. And while driving back from the cemetery after we'd buried the Reverend, I recalled a priceless Sunday morning at Ebenezer when he'd been the subject of some whispers along the front pews as several schoolteachers attending services began snickering and exchanging cutting remarks about the pastor's grammar. He'd responded by saying to one of them that during the time the church was raising its building fund several years back, "I have give a hundred dollars while the man with the good speech have give nothin'!" I remembered that story as Bunch and I drove home. And I laughed very softly to myself until my eyes were filled with tears.

Eight

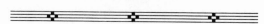

After the death of Reverend Williams, I was called to the pastorate of Ebenezer. I did not accept the call immediately because I was still committed to Traveler's Rest. Moreover, though I was no stranger to Ebenezer, some of the deacons felt that an older and more experienced pastor should succeed Reverend Williams. As I had done, and would continue to do with all my major decisions, I began praying that God would guide me in the direction that He wanted me to go. I aspired to pastor a large church, but I did not want to accept one before God told me I was ready to assume more responsibilities and a larger role of leadership.

I knew that Reverend Williams had worked arduously to bring Ebenezer to the prominent place that it occupied in the lives of the members and in the Atlanta community. Surely, for his memory, for the sakes of my wife, my mother-in-law, and the members, I wanted the church to continue to grow and thrive. But most of all, I wanted what was best for Ebenezer. Ebenezer did not belong to us. It belonged to God and His work on earth. Naturally, I now felt a very strong bond to the church

—the members were our extended family—but I would be guided by God.

Now, I knew my wife was also praying for my guidance, but I began to think that her prayer may have been, "Lord, don't direct King to Ebenezer."

Bunch was "born" in Ebenezer. Except for the Sundays she spent with me at Traveler's Rest after our marriage, she had never known another church. At Traveler's Rest she was Mrs. King. Although she was now married, at Ebenezer she was still "Lil" Alberta or Alberta.

"King," she said, "I don't want you to go to Ebenezer. I'll never be the First Lady there, but at Traveler's Rest I am the First Lady." Well, I thought I understood how Bunch felt, and I was sympathetic to her, but when I received my answer from God, I knew that I should accept Ebenezer's call. I said to her, "We are going to Ebenezer and you will continue to work there as you did when your father was the pastor. We'll build our legacy at Ebenezer; new members will join. And, as those who have known you since you were born become older and leave us, you will have a new generation that will not have known "Lil" Alberta or your mother. They will know only Mrs. King, the First Lady of Ebenezer.

I became the pastor of Ebenezer in the fall of 1931, and I was correct about Bunch's role in my pastorate. She was a peerless co-worker in the continuing growth of Ebenezer. She endeared herself to the hundreds of members who joined the church during my administration. And, as I had told her she would, with the passage of time and her incomparable contributions to the church, she earned her place in the hearts of the members as the First Lady of Ebenezer Baptist Church.

The board of deacons of the church was not pleased at first. They felt an older, more experienced man was needed to pastor the church in those difficult times. But Mrs. Williams, who had maintained a quiet but very solid position of influence at Ebenezer during all the years her husband was minister, put all the objections to rest when she told the congregation one Sunday morning that in her view, I was going to be the church's new leader.

I felt that even in the middle of the Depression a wonderful moment had come to my life in the form of great promise and hope for the future. Just weeks later, though, I had cause to wonder.

A realty company held a mortgage on the Ebenezer church building. When the company went bankrupt, late in 1931, the Atlanta Federal Savings Bank took over our note, which had an outstanding balance of $1,100. Because the realty company hadn't been making its payments, the bank moved in to seize all its assets. I arrived one morning to open the church and found that our doors had been padlocked. The marshals were just leaving. We hadn't been notified, there had been no warning. They just locked us out.

I went downtown and talked to the bank manager. Atlanta Federal had no real interest in our building. As a piece of real estate, its main value was the one Ebenezer Church gave it as a house of worship. The bank manager was an impatient fellow, and he obviously had been listening to hard-luck tales all that day. People all over the city were really up against it financially.

"We can pay off the mortgage," I assured him, though at the time I didn't know for sure. If things got any worse for the Ebenezer folks, money would be tighter than ever before. They were giving until it hurt them. Asking them to sacrifice even more to save our building wasn't going to be pleasant.

But the bank manager was willing to work out a payment schedule with me. And as poor as we were then, the note, which ran for five more years, was paid off in three and a half. We did more than survive. A deep sense of pride filled the church now. Our Sunday mornings had a joy about them, a passion in the songs, and a pleasure in the pastor's sermons that came from knowing what strength people could bring to hardship, what faith and fellowship. I knew that throughout the congregation there were people who went without meals to keep money in our collection plates.

And I preached that we wouldn't just make it through but we would prosper, because this belief of ours was something special. "Ebenezer will give this world much that is special," I said, "because we walk any path proudly. We can be weary but continue on without a word of reproach. And we will, church," I preached. "We surely will."

And eventually we did prosper. The deacons, twelve in all, got together and gave the church $25 each to form a building fund. I had asked them each to contribute twenty dollars. They not only gave themselves but raised money on their jobs and among friends and relatives. They even managed to raise my salary just a year after I became Ebenezer's pastor. The deacons took great pride in knowing that young Reverend King was the best-paid Negro minister in the city. The black church in America has always honored its ministry, but I was treated extraordinarily well by Ebenezer. In return, I worked to give my congregation a continuing sense of our strength as God had provided it. We had been asked by Him to bear a great burden in our time. But we could rise above any misery and grief. Others might slip under the weight, Ebenezer determined not to. So many of us had come from places where Negroes were not regarded as part of the human race. We knew better. And we knew that in time everyone else in this country would understand our struggle, our patience, our anger, and our spiritual power to change not only our own condition but that of the rest of this nation. Nothing would ever overwhelm us. We could be set back, knocked down, and kicked around. But we'd live. And in our living, America would discover its future.

Family became my anchor. Being a parent often seemed rather strange. I remained accustomed to thinking of myself as a son long after I'd left my father's house. And as my children grew, I became more familiar with what Mama and Papa had been talking about when they'd seemed a little harsh with us. To prepare a child for a world where death and violence are always near drains a lot of energy from the soul. Inside you, there is always a fist balled up to protect them. And a constant sense of the hard line between maintaining self-respect and getting along with the enemy all around you. In the Southern Railroad Yards, I had watched men betray one another to get on the good side of the bosses, never realizing that the good side had nothing to do with victory. And now, as I grew within the increasingly influential world of the southern black church, I wondered how much would be expected of me as a person who presumably had arrived somewhere better, somewhere higher and nicer, within the framework of the segregated society. What would my own children expect of me when they understood the part of the world we occupied? The central question was whether the forces opposed to the aspirations of the Negro community would defeat us, would leave us willing to accept the status of lesser beings. Could we simply go along with the system that rewarded silence and apparent agreement by making a few creature comforts available to those willing to forget what the real issues actually were?

Ebenezer was prospering, but I often wondered if the cost of our survival was higher than it seemed to be. Separate societies, as a practical matter, cost the taxpayers much more than any human vanity was ever worth. How much does the citizen pay for two drinking fountains—for white and for colored—and two school systems, double public facilities in every conceivable area of public life? One system is cheaper, one is right, one is human.

In this South I lived in during the early 1930s, all actions, all viewpoints, all morality, justice, and true faith were manifest among the South's people in one word: nigger. What this term represented to each man, woman, and child, whatever their color, told, finally, the story of America. There was anguish in white homes. I had seen and sensed it as a boy, going to back doors, waiting for my mother to scrub other people's floors, listening to whites hate us without them or us knowing why. Whites ached. And sadly, some of them thought keeping their heels on our heads could make them feel a little better, or a little safer, or a little closer to God. But nobody can keep a slave without being a slave, too. Visitors to the South would often comment on how harmoniously these segregated tribes of people seemed to live right next to each other. But the smoldering resentments were there, as anyone who's ever been called "nigger" can explain. Resentment that also came from hearing people say that the Negro didn't want his condition changed in the South. The happy darky was a myth held on to by folks who never learned to face the truth.

There is a difference between the person who is still waiting for freedom and the person who has finished waiting and wants something *done*. The South needed more time, whites kept on saying. Things will definitely change in just a little while. Some blacks waited a lifetime on that false promise because the more powerful white voices in the South belonged to men who were demagogues: the Talmadges, the Longs, and the Bilbos, men who formed alliances *against* change, against the possibility of racial harmony. The Negro in the South had been asking: When? And the supposedly reasonable white southerners kept saying: Soon. But the political forces that controlled the entire region of the old Confederacy really meant: Never!

And so the Negro continued to be an easy target of hatred, a "thing" to be kept in its place, to be despised, brutalized, or killed. We, in turn, were not fighting out of hatred for anybody. Our struggle was not so much against other people as it was against the systems people had created to keep us from living decent lives. Whites could only hate *us*. We had no political machinery or systems to oppress them. We had no signs to represent who we thought we were. Negroes did not divide buses by race or build separate drinking fountains. The police did not support our prejudices with the force of guns. We were vulnerable. Our victories and losses in the civil-rights struggle had to begin with that understanding.

I became a chronic complainer. I grumbled about all the conditions I saw segregation imposing on Negroes, and I talked too loud about it at times and got on a lot of people's nerves. A few folks said my Morehouse degree had added a few inches to my hat size. But every time I saw Negroes using separate water fountains or shuffling toward the backs of buses, I wondered why some reasonable whites and blacks couldn't just sit down and bring a swift halt to all of the dumb kinds of things segregation represented. But I was told by more than a few Negroes to stop grandstanding about the racial situation in Atlanta because it was pretty damn good compared to a lot of places, and we should just be satisfied with it until whites could see their way clear to work with us on some changes.

Well, I'd get so riled up at statements like this that Bunch would have to use all her considerable skills of reasoning with me to get my temperature back down. Even when that happened, I felt I was right. *We* would have to change things. Whites were not interested in change. The only change most of them wanted to see was Reverend Martin Luther King keeping his mouth shut about conditions for Negroes in the South. But Reverend King just wasn't going to do that, because Reverend King just wasn't satisfied with the way things were in the South.

And I intended to keep on complaining.

Oddly enough, this was a period of enormous growth for Ebenezer. The church's membership continued to increase. My salary now had increased considerably. Bunch and the kids and I had material comforts in our home, and we had the spiritual warmth of Ebenezer in our lives.

In 1934, I traveled to Europe and the Middle East. I traveled with a party of ten other ministers from around the United States. We arrived in France by ship, went down through Italy by train, traveled over onto the continent of Africa, across Tunisia, Libya, and Egypt, then finally on to Palestine and the Holy Land. In Jerusalem, when I saw with my own eyes the places where Jesus had lived and taught, a life spent in the ministry seemed to me even more compelling.

Returning to Europe, we all attended a World Baptist Conference in Berlin, Germany. For a week I heard the broadcasts of a man on the radio who seemed—although I understood no German—to shriek and roar, as if he wanted everyone who heard him to rise up and follow. I heard rage in that voice; it was a sound I'd heard in my own language too many times, a sound that poured oil on roaring flames. Adolf Hitler was on the rise, and the week we spent in Germany was filled with the sight of his image on posters and of streets filled with soldiers, with the sound of his voice seemingly everywhere day and night. It was difficult to imagine, somehow, that in this same city was a huge convention of Baptists from all over the world, praying, hoping, feeling that we could take back home, some of us, a new sense of how peace was to be accomplished among men. Simultaneously the militaristic march of jackboots continued beneath unfurling flags with swastikas emblazoned on them. Perhaps both sides were convinced that they had the right answers for tomorrow.

Visiting the Holy Land was very nourishing spiritually, but

it did not reduce my concern about the South entirely. Still, I was refreshed by the many new worlds I had an opportunity to visit.

I began uncovering the mysteries of the South's racial *arrangement* around 1935. Negroes and whites had been placed into a framework, a design that separated them by color, and for far too many people in both groups the terms of segregation had become acceptable as a social tradition. For many people there was simply no other way to live. And as a part of all this, I'd become a prosperous young pastor, a husband and father whose family had never lived in a rented home or driven a car on which a payment was ever made late. We dressed well, we ate well, we enjoyed great respect among the people of our community. Perhaps this should always have been enough, but it never was. The southern arrangement was as destructive as it was often superficially charming to outsiders, to those who had come to see the South as a gallant defender of some fine and noble way of life.

Part of the protective covering put around this dehumanizing system—and it should be clear that segregation dehumanized both sides—was the creation of apparent privilege for certain sectors of the Negro population in the South. I had been, for instance, a registered voter for more than ten years before I fully realized that my access to this franchise had value only in relationship to the number of other black people who were utilizing their voting rights.

My vote alone would mean nothing until social and political change could be more than a vision of a distant future. I organized a few meetings and sounded out a few close friends, among them several other Atlanta churchmen. There were arguments, healthy kinds of disagreement in the beginning. Eventually, though, I began to sense the formation of a strong opinion based, for the most part, on the theory that the comfortable passenger is the last one who should think about rocking the boat. Still, I felt that action was the only course for those of us whose relative financial security permitted a view of the overall situation that wasn't entirely available—or practical—for folks whose very livelihoods could depend on the sort of smiles I'd once learned to display in the Southern Railway Yards. Any grinning I did now was on my own terms, and I'd come to feel that a certain responsibility went along with that very small freedom to be what I wanted to be.

At one of these meetings I proposed that black churches become central headquarters for a voter drive that would be kicked off by a march to City Hall, where hundreds of black Atlantans would register en masse.

The idea fell on deaf ears. When any of my fellow clergy spoke, it was to suggest that I keep such notions to myself, there was far too much at stake for Negroes in Atlanta to risk anything over some actions that could only bring trouble. Some others made the point that there was no need for everybody in the black community to vote as long as those who knew what government was really all about exercised that right wisely for themselves and for those folks who attended church.

In fact, this was a widespread view among blacks and whites. It was an arrangement: Negro ministers would speak to the whites and get from them the message that was to be delivered among the citizens of the city's Negro communities. As long as everyone did his job, there didn't ever have to be any trouble. What was arranged, then, was a system of very real favors. But like all favors, they could be taken away more quickly than they had been offered, they were based in no genuine sense of mutual respect, and they had nothing to do with *rights*. For the Negro in the South, voting power represented the only way favors were going to be turned into the inalienable rights that the United States supposedly guaranteed all people.

I even had trouble with the deacons of Ebenezer on my plan for a voting-rights march. But they were not about to go to the members against the wishes of the pastor who'd built this grand church even larger than it had been, and who was determined to see that it kept right on growing.

Most church folks in Atlanta knew that not every young minister was so successful in keeping his pastorate in such stable economic shape as I was. So I was able to persuade the deacons, with the minimum of encouragement actually, to support my drive to enlist people for the rally and the march.

Of course, there were a few members who were not overly

enthusiastic, either. But some of them fortunately could be reminded of the padlock that had gone on Ebenezer's door in 1931, and had come off so shortly thereafter, and the food and clothes that had been so helpful in the lives of so many in Atlanta. The majority of the membership encouraged the reluctant to have faith in a young minister's judgment on this particular matter.

We started out with a rally in Ebenezer, explaining to all who were participating just what kind of behavior we expected during the entire action on that day. When we left the church, for all Atlanta knew we were just a bunch of Negro church folks heading out of town to a picnic.

More than a thousand people had gathered for the rally at Ebenezer, and several ministers, myself included, told the crowd that we were not stirring up trouble, but we were tired of waiting for the freedoms America said were every citizen's right. I reminded those at the rally of how things had been for me and for many of them out in the country, where talk of rights and the law seemed to lead us into constant trouble. Now we were all looking for a new way. "I know one thing," I shouted. "I ain't gonna plow no more mules. I'll never step off the road again to let white folks pass. I am going to move forword toward freedom, and I'm hoping everybody here today is going right along with me!"

People began shouting so loud over what I was saying, I wasn't sure whether they were with or against me. But we all went outside together, and I knew then that my enthusiasm was matched by that of hundreds of other people, some of whom had been unable to squeeze inside the church for the rally but had taken their places in the march line as we formed up and started out for City Hall.

We soon found that with relatives and friends and tithing members and a few supporters from the other Negro churches in town, there were several hundred Negro Americans marching that afternoon in 1935, down to the Atlanta City Hall, in a demonstration such as no living soul in that city had ever seen. People along the streets looked on in amazement as we went along in straight, orderly rows, headed downtown. Some of them knew of the rallies Reverend Williams had organized in the early 1920s, when he stopped a municipal bond issue in its tracks because it contained no provisions for Negro high-school education. The result of that had been Booker T. Washington High School, opened in 1924, the first high school for black students in Atlanta.

"Lawd, they marchin' again," I heard more than one person lining the way call out. And I yelled back a dozen or more times, every few blocks: "Yes, and you come on 'n' march with us, brother; walk with us, sister . . ."

Truly, we lived out the word: Walk together, children, don't get weary—in that early time, when the police stood and watched, some of them dumbfounded, most of them with their eyes turned into steel and their jaws bulging hatred; back in that early time, when nobody saw reports of marches in the newspapers because the newspapers did not want, in any way, to encourage Negroes in that sort of behavior. And Negroes went inside City Hall, and into that elevator that we would not be rid of for some years to come, and they became partners in the business of America.

A lot marched, but, of course, not all of them registered. Maybe a couple of hundred out of the crowd did. But it was a great start, I remember thinking, a really fine beginning. It was a day of great pride, a day when the very ministers who had said no so forcefully in our meetings just happened to be in the neighborhood, after our march had gone a mile without incident. They joined in under the banners that proclaimed that we were starting to move forward into another day, another way. We were staring at freedom, and though the picture wasn't entirely clear, all of us knew what we wanted to see one day, and where we wanted to be when we did.

Days later, sitting in my study at Ebenezer, I tried to weigh the effect of the rally and the march. Eventually the point had been made, and emphatically. But I realized also that, in the actions Reverend Williams had taken years earlier, there had been very specific results: Booker T. Washington High School and the first Negro branch of the YMCA, victories that might have seemed slight to an outsider. But to every southerner, black or white, these things called to mind points on a historical map. Sometimes they'd be swept under rugs, kept there, patted down, until these victories were taken for granted, as if they had always been there, as though no one had given a great deal to obtain them. Negroes built the Butler Street Y in Atlanta with money raised in the Negro community. Only after the building was finished would the national organization give us a charter. We were given little, if anything; we gained for ourselves, without question, a great deal.

Our great sense of frustration, in virtually every area of the South where Negroes lived, came from feeling, at times, that the world we knew should exist might not appear in time for us to see even a part of it.

Nine

As early as the 1930s, though not at any time before that, the
South might have addressed and solved the nation's racial
dilemma. But this would have required a leadership the South
did not really ever develop—leadership among white clergymen.
Every effort that Negro churchmen made toward not only a
reconciliation but a progressive unity within the framework of
southern religious life was rejected. There were simply no white
ministers who would run the risk of meeting with us because
such gatherings would have to be meetings between equals.
The spiritual prison of segregated life was so strong that even
the most powerful white minister would have lost his congregation for suggesting that the races were, in the sight of God,
equals. If this implies that southern whites felt stronger in their
faith in racial separation than in their belief in the possibility
of racial harmony, the record speaks clearly. From the white
Baptist churches of the South—and they were and remain the
most influential institutions in this part of the country—no one
emerged to look at the human condition as it was in the South
and to say: Enough, this will come to an end because it con-
tradicts every part of the Bible and all the doctrine and prin-

ciples that book contains. We sought out a leader from the white community, feeling that if even one would speak, a new mood could be created here. We discovered that in this instance seeking brought nothing. And so we waited, feeling that across the huge but senseless divide, *someone* from the large, heavily populated other side would stand up and be counted, even if just one. It did not happen.

The terms of the struggle during that period were harsh and coldly efficient. To change what needed to be changed required a solid effort across the country, not just in the South. But the only conclusion we could draw was that we were, in the most terrible way, alone. The newspapers did not use their massive power to influence—except, for many years, to discredit—what Negroes were trying to do in gaining rights already assured us by the U.S. Constitution. The great historians and social scientists of the day went along with the most primitive conclusions about Negro life and the contributions of darker people to world history. Everywhere in this country and many places around the world, we found ourselves boxed in by hosts of antagonistic forces. And so a great many people were discouraged. Some simply stopped trying, moving into the embrace of segregation as something representing the "very best we can do right now."

During the summer of 1936, I opened our house to several meetings held by an organization of Negro schoolteachers who wanted to find a way to protest pay scales established for them. There was, of course, another, higher scale offered white teachers with the same qualifications and experience. This was one of the more blatant examples of discrimination, and the teachers felt certain the time had come to turn all this around and achieve equalization of pay for all, regardless of color.

I hadn't planned to participate as anything more than an observer and host for the first planning meetings. But it was soon clear that leadership in this fight was going to have to come from outside the teaching profession. Too much pressure could be applied to the teachers themselves, all of whom held their jobs without any real security or anything even resembling tenure. There had been firings before in the school system, over lesser matters than protests or organizing. As a minister with a growing church family, I simply wasn't in the same position the teachers occupied. They were vulnerable to pressures I didn't have to consider. Nobody was going to fire me from the pulpit; my voice could be heard and would be. I didn't fear any reprisals, either. So I chaired the fight by these teachers, and it was a fight, more than just a group effort to accomplish something reasonable. Perhaps if I'd known that eleven years would pass before equality and, basically, respect was achieved for Negro teachers, my enthusiasm might have cooled down a little. I like to think not.

In the beginning, things got a little rough. Few outside the South understood in those days how much emotional heat really was stirred up by racial questions. Just a couple of days after the first teachers' meeting was held in my home, a white minister called on me at Ebenezer to express his concern. It was his feeling that I just didn't know how much opposition would be mounted against us, and how dangerous that opposition might prove. In a way he was right. Over several weeks I received dozens of hate letters, as word got around that Negro teachers, led by Ebenezer's pastor, were fighting for some very fundamental rights as citizens. Drawings of me in a coffin were popular in these letters, as were ones of my neck being stretched by a rope. Several white ministers called on me after that, each expressing concern, each maintaining that his own congregation was too emotional on the issue for him to take a stand other than the popular one: that niggers should stay in their places if they wanted peace to prevail in the South.

But in a larger sense, our difficulty in Atlanta had much to do with factionalism and division within the black community. Quite often this hampered efforts to seize the time. During the Depression, the teachers had been stunned in many instances to find out how other Negroes lived all the time. Vividly I recall the desperation of those who were laid off from any kind of jobs; but the teachers especially were hard hit, because it seemed as though all their training and professional preparation just flew out the window, sending them to soup lines where they rubbed shoulders with folks who'd never known what a steady job was.

My efforts in bringing church men and women outside Ebenezer into this struggle ran aground time and again because when churches pull together for anything, the question of leadership, of just who will run the ship, becomes an immediate, primary concern. So between poor folks thinking the teachers were elite, middle-class brats, and ministers refusing to join me in a clearly moral question, enough conflict for twice eleven years stood squarely before us.

There were teachers, for instance, who thought the whole matter could be resolved in a few days with some phone calls and a small delegation meeting with city officials. But this was a time when city governments in the South kept themselves so far away from Negro concerns that City Hall could have as easily been located on the moon. I thought the problem could be overcome fairly easily if teachers would confront certain facts. Registering to vote, which not all of them rushed to do, seemed to me a powerful lever to pull in any situation. But again, Reverend King wasn't going to be laid off from his place in the pulpit because he was a voter. Teachers feared that possibility, however, and I was not going to diminish that fear with words.

It was during the late Thirties that some people in Atlanta, including a few of my fellow members of the Negro clergy, began to look upon my activities and concerns as being more than strange. And so, more than once, I heard men I considered close, longtime friends tell me: Look, King, there's no need rocking any boats and getting these white folks upset. A lot of us have some good things going for ourselves, and we can help some of our less fortunate brethren, but it'll take time, years, maybe, because we've got to go slow.

But we can create political power and bring about those changes we want quickly, I found myself saying over and over, privately, to friends, and in meetings where I was often greeted with silence, eyes cast down, church fans fluttering away, not much open support.

Some attitudes among people are difficult to overcome; others just never go away. So many times I heard Negroes say to each other: "Well, hell, there's nothing you can do about the way things are until *they* decide the time has come. The white man owns everything, and he's gonna run things his own way until he gets downright tired of it, and that's bound to take at least another million years!"

I argued, I shouted, some people thought I acted up, but these kinds of sentiments just angered me more than I should have allowed. No initiative to end segregation and the bigotry it helped maintain would emerge from the white community. Any actions that produced change would have to come from the Negro community. And then only if leadership was developed on a larger scale and respected and followed as well. White support, if it ever came, would be welcome, but depending on it made for a fool's errand. What few Negroes knew and few seldom talked about was the incredible pressure whites could be subjected to when any of them chose even to discuss the notion that men and women of all colors were human beings, not more and not less, and that this was something God, not man, took respsonsibility for. Whites who leaned toward understanding and brotherhood could be made to suffer, their businesses shut down, burned, wrecked by hoodlums. Or their children could be ostracized in school, or made to feel like freaks with no place in a "normal society." For a white person to support our struggle required more strength than most folks had. But for the Negro, the struggle had no escape hatches; only whites could quit.

There were constant reminders of just how widespread and how evil segregation actually was. Negroes who considered themselves well off in terms of social station or economic security had only to go into downtown Atlanta to discover again just how little those things meant in a racist environment. In fact, a grim little joke about this often made the rounds of Negro gatherings as a brief, pointed reminder of what we were all up against. Blacks would pose the question to one another in a whisper: "What do white folks call a Negro who's got a Ph.D., a new home, and a fine automobile, along with lots of money in the bank?" Answer: "A nigger." I had no problem remembering what segregation meant. Instances of it surrounded me.

When M.L. was six years old, I took him downtown with me, and we enjoyed a very pleasant ride in the family car. In those days we seldom shopped outside the Negro business community, but on one of the bigger streets near the center of town, M.L. spotted a pair of shoes in a window and asked me to buy them. Well, he needed a pair, and so we went inside the store where the shoes he liked so much were displayed. A clerk appeared as soon as we stepped past the door and very coldly announced that we should go to the back of the store where he'd help us in just a few minutes. I told him we were quite comfortable in the front of the store, and if he didn't want to sell us any shoes there, we wouldn't be buying any.

The young clerk's face reddened. He insisted again that we go in the back, the way all Negroes who came in there were happy to do. No exceptions. No exceptions were ever made to this rule, he told me. "You take it like everybody else, and stop being so high and mighty!" M.L. was looking up at me. I could see he was confused by what was going on. After all, he only wanted a pair of shoes to wear. When I told him we were leaving, he seemed ready to cry. In trying to explain, I became angry—not at him, but the little fella didn't know that and became very frightened. As we drove back toward Auburn Avenue, I was able to speak quietly about the whole episode in the store, but the questions, the confusions, remained in his eyes.

This was the ridiculous nature of segregation in the South. A grown man could make no sense of it to a very bright six-year-old boy. M.L. just couldn't understand why it was all right to buy shoes in the back part of a store and not in the front. Because people come in so many different colors in the Negro community, it was hard for him to figure out how anybody could use the color of a person's skin to separate him from others. In M.L.'s world, some Negroes looked white. Others were very dark, still others fitted somewhere in between. Why would anybody have an advantage over others on this basis? And who really knew whether some folks were white or Negro, just on the basis of what their skin color *seemed* to reveal?

M.L. stared at me in the car and asked me to explain the whole thing again. And I said to him that the best way to explain it was to say that I'd never accept the stupidity and cruelty of segregation, not as long as I lived. I was going to be fighting against it in some way or other as long as there was breath in me. I wanted him to understand *that*. He still looked puzzled. But he nodded his head and told me that if I was against it, he would help me all he could. And I remember smiling and telling him how much I appreciated his support. He was such a little fellow then, but sitting there next to me in the car, M.L. seemed so thoughtful and determined on this matter that I felt certain he wouldn't forget his promise to help.

Bunch's mother, Mrs. Jennie Celeste Williams, passed away on May 18, 1941. M.L. was hit especially hard by her death. He'd slipped away to watch a parade when he was supposed to be studying. And when he got back, he discovered that his grandmother had gone on home to glory. M.L. thought God was punishing the family for his "sin" of having gone out of the house without telling anyone. He cried off and on for several days afterward, and was unable to sleep at night. I sat in the bedroom he and A.D. shared, explaining for nearly all of an afternoon that God wasn't that angry about M.L. neglecting a little homework or going to see a parade. Death, I told my sons, was a part of life that was difficult to get used to, no matter how many times it visited our families or those we knew. "Don't blame what has happened to your grandmother on anything you've done," I told M.L. "God has His own plan and His own way, and we cannot change or interfere with the time He chooses to call any of us back to Him."

Later that year I moved the family to a large yellow brick home (which had been owned by a Negro doctor) on Boulevard, only a few blocks from where we had lived. This was the kind of house I had been dreaming about since the first time I ran away from the country, shaking my fist at the house where my little white friend Jay lived. I would never forget how embarrassed I was one day when Jay and I were playing together and went to his house, a large red brick one, and I was told, "You can't come in the front door."

I vowed then that one day I would own a brick house, and now I owned one—larger and finer than the one in Stockbridge. Earlier, I made an effort to buy that house Jay had lived in (when he was grown, he owned a lot of property around Stockbridge). I gave him $500 earnest money, but Jay gave me the money back several weeks later. I learned that his wife worried that folks around Stockbridge wouldn't think too highly of a Negro who'd grown up there as a sharecropper's son coming back to buy one of the biggest "white" houses in town.

Once I saw the house on Boulevard, none of that business with Jay bothered me anymore, although I'd been very angry when it had happened. The South had simply reminded me again that Negro people, even if they prospered and could afford to buy certain things, were still to be refused many of them on the basis of color.

The area around Boulevard was a comfortable residential community. Negroes who lived there were by no means fabulously wealthy as some people in other parts of Atlanta imagined. The black middle class worked hard. But as economic security was being achieved, it was often necessary to withstand certain jealousies that arose *within* the black community, where success by some was often greeted with mixed emotion by others. There were Negroes who believed that a black person with anything couldn't have gotten it honestly, that is, without selling out his soul to whites, "tomming," betraying his brothers in the ghetto.

During the late 1930s, black and white leaders began meeting fairly regularly to discuss mutual roles in maintaining what whites liked to call the "excellent" race relations in our city. A few of us in the Negro community felt these informal gatherings could have been more constructive if everyone involved had been committed to basic social change. But whites were fond of claiming that patience was all Negroes needed to weather a storm that would surely end . . . sometime, as every storm does.

In 1940, Dr. Benjamin E. Mays was the new president of Morehouse College. He wasted no time letting whites in power know that he felt enormous pride in being part of a city with the will to be great. Whites were pleased to hear what they considered an endorsement of the status quo. But Dr. Mays was very much in favor of change. He was also a scholar of considerable reputation, and a compelling orator. Whites in government and business began to listen. Dr. Mays, in turn, called for a wider dialogue between white and Negro Atlanta. A small coalition formed. But very little came out of the initial meetings. There was an uneasiness as two wary groups circled each other verbally. Although Atlanta was at that time one of the South's most segregated cities, the white businessmen who met with us saw little need to interfere with the "gracious Atlanta way of doing things."

I joined with several prominent members of Atlanta's Negro leadership in creating our part of the coalition. My neighbor John Wesley Dobbs; Dr. Mays; A. T. Walden, an attorney; and C. A. Scott, publisher of the *Atlanta Daily World*, were all family men with careers to consider. But freedom had special meaning to all of us. Walden had fought the Klan as a young man in rural Georgia. Now he was prominent in the NAACP as a legal counsel. Walden knew how hard-headed crackers could be, and how violent they could be on the subject of race. He knew how to fight on more than one level, toe-to-toe with enemies who forced him to that method, and also reasonably, with a knowledgeable use of the legal apparatus available to all Americans. Dobbs was a shrewd negotiator, able and quite outspoken. C. A. Scott was a successful businessman whose newspaper was one of several enterprises operated by his family. Scott, above all, was an American who believed deeply in this country and its people. He did not believe in activism in the sense of public demonstrations. Leaders, he felt, should handle problems among themselves, make decisions, and pass them along to the public.

My view, though I certainly didn't avoid acting in a leadership capacity, was that the masses had to take part in social change. Voter registration drives, in which I believed strongly, were only part of that involvement. The picket line, in my opinion, was the best weapon we had. Certainly it meant bringing folks out into the streets. True, it invited opposition from those whites who became crazed over the possibility of "race-mixing." But this kind of action had an effect on a vital part of our city's life—its economy.

Atlanta, of course, was always the South's center of finance, trade, and transportation. Its large middle class, both black and white, was separated by old and useless laws instead of being joined by many mutual interests: regard for family life, for church, education, and law-abiding citizenship. Instead of growing into what it might have been—the finest and most completely American city in the nation—Atlanta allowed the narrow interests of some of its people to dominate the good sense and charitable spirit of others. The business community had always been a solid force that controlled Atlanta's political and social destiny. Any change that affected the city's economic, social or political atmosphere had to come through the businessmen; their point of view was always crucial.

But the business community, though very dynamic in its quests for new markets and increased profits, did not always spend that much passion and energy on the cause of human freedom. Businessmen were pathetically slow in Atlanta when it came to using their refined mechanisms, so good for making money, to achieve some sense of purpose in life beyond dollars and cents. The moral issue within the business community in the South always started and ended with segregation. White Christians could not read a Bible that said ". . . what you do unto the least of my brethren you do unto me," and sense that God was watching the South and asking for courage from white folks as well as black. On the issue of racial discrimination, there was *no* white leadership at all. Black leaders operated in a vacuum. Whites were only maintaining a holding action, trying to see how much they could get away with and for how long. The political economy of segregation made it a difficult system to oppose. Negro wages were lower than white wages. Negroes were strictly confined to certain neighborhoods. Slick businessmen made a lot of money from situations like that, as they have all over America throughout the twentieth century. Things were controlled. The poor, black and white, were taught to hate each other. Businessmen made money from both sides and used the controls of segregation to create an economy that always brought advantage to them. With so much money involved, none of them was about to change this. And so there was no leadership among the businessmen, who were so powerful in Atlanta. And when the powerful have no leaders, everybody is in trouble, because a lot of mediocre people begin

(*Top left*) My father, James Albert King, in the early 1920's. (*Top right*) Me at twenty-two years of age. (*Middle left*) My father-in-law, the Reverend Adam Daniel Williams, in the backyard of his home at 501 Auburn Avenue, in northeast Atlanta, in the 1920's. (*Middle right*) My graduation picture when I completed my work at Morehouse College, 1930. (*Lower left*) The family in January, 1939. Seated are (*left to right*) A.D., Christine, and M.L. Mrs. King (*left*), I, and my mother-in-law, Mrs. Jeannie C. Parks Williams, are standing. (*Lower right*) This is how I looked in the 1940's.

(*Above*) I am with the Sunday school in celebration of the sixtieth anniversary of Ebenezer Baptist Church and my fifteenth anniversary as pastor of the church, 1947. (*Left*) With M.L. on Commencement Day at Morehouse College in Atlanta, 1948. (*Below*) Christine, Bunch, A.D., and I with M.L. at his graduation from Crozer Seminary in June, 1951. His friend and classmate, the Reverend Walter McCall (now deceased), is kneeling in front.

Bunch and I cut our twenty-fifth wedding anniversary cake in November, 1951.

On April 12, 1959, A.D. was installed as the pastor of Vernon First Baptist Church in Newnan, Georgia, and M.L. and I were participants in the Installation Service.

(*Above left*) Bunch, Christine, A.D., Coretta, and I are with M.L., who is holding the Nobel Peace Prize gold medal, which was presented to him earlier in the day, December 10, 1964. Coretta is holding the case which contains the Nobel diploma. (*Moneta Sleet, Jr.*/Ebony *magazine*) (*Above right*) A grand reception was held for M.L. in the 369th Regimental Armory in New York City when we returned from the Nobel Peace Prize ceremonies. With Juanita Abernathy, Governor and Mrs. Nelson Rockefeller of New York, and Dorothy Height, I am singing the anthem of the Movement, "We Shall Overcome." (Ebony *magazine*) (*Below*) I am convincing (?) Bunch of a point in my study at Ebenezer in the spring of 1968.

This picture was taken shortly after I viewed M.L.'s body lying in state in Atlanta. My daughter, Christine, is with me. (*Wide World Photos*)

My brothers James, Henry, Joel and I, with our sisters, Mrs. Cleo Hill, Mrs. Lenora Walker, and Mrs. Woodie Brown, 1972.

(*Right*) My grandchildren on the steps: Mrs. Alveda King Ellis, Alfred D. W. King II, Derek B. King, Yolanda D. King, Esther Darlene King, Martin Luther King III, Vernon Christopher King, Isaac Farris, Jr., and to his right, Dexter Scott King. Kneeling in front are Isaac's sister, Angela Christine Farris (*left*), and his cousin Bernice Albertine King. Standing: Naomi King, my daughter-in-law; Isaac and Christine Farris, my son-in-law and daughter; Coretta King, my daughter-in-law; and my wife, Mrs. Alberta King. I am holding our great-grandson, Jarrett Ellis, in our home, December, 1972. (*Count Jackson*) (*Below left*) Eddie Clifford Beal III. (*Below right*) Darlene Ruth Celeste Beal.

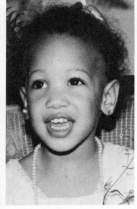

(*Opposite left*) Governor George Busbee of Georgia proclaimed August 1, 1975, the day of my retirement from the pastorate of Ebenezer Baptist Church, "Martin Luther King, Sr., Day" in Georgia. With me in his office to receive the proclamation are my granddaughter Angela Farris; my daughter, Christine Farris; my sister Woodie Brown; my grandson Martin Luther III; daughter-in-law Coretta King; granddaughter Bernice King; and grandsons Dexter King (behind Bernice) and Isaac Farris, Jr. (*Top*) The sanctuary of Ebenezer Baptist Church in Atlanta, Georgia, where I pastored for more than forty years. (*Above*) I delivered the benediction at the closing session of the 1976 Democratic National Convention in New York City. (*Edward Hausner/NYT Pictures*)

(*Left*) President Carter introduced me when I delivered the 113th anniversary sermon at Zion Baptist Church in Washington, D.C. The little girl could not be restrained from shaking the President's hand. September, 1977. (*Wide World Photos*)
(*Below left*) When this photo of me was taken in October, 1977, I had just been "checking up" on President Carter, commenting on the job he had done thus far for black people and on the work he still had to do, as I saw it. (*Wide World Photos*)
(*Below right*) In October, 1979, Morehouse College's School of Religion held a dinner in my honor at the Washington Hilton Hotel. With me in this photo are Coretta and Christine. (*Wide World Photos*)

to twist and turn and manipulate a society in the absence of strong, dynamic and, above all, reasonable voices.

In terms of the moral climate among any people, the direction provided by society's visionary people is vital. Like the businessmen, Atlanta's white clergy was without a true leader who could have influenced thousands of people to change before the crisis became more serious. No one came forth.

Only one white politician made what I still consider the most sincere effort of that time. And if he hadn't been alone so much of the time, his name might be even better known outside the South.

William B. Hartsfield was an Atlanta lawyer who entered local politics during the late 1930s. He brought with him an unusual campaign style and a very astute sense of the direction in which the South was then headed. Before Hartsfield ran for mayor, Negroes had been ignored by the candidates in Atlanta's municipal elections. Because of the white primary system, which barred us from participating in state and city politics, the only real contact Negroes had with elected officials or candidates for public office came through the occasional and informal meetings held between white and black leaders. The role of the Negro in these talks was strictly advisory. We depended on the goodwill of whites because no actual power was then in our hands, unless you consider the power to disrupt through demonstrations.

When Hartsfield made his bid for mayor in 1946, he had a reputation that brought him scorn from whites and some admiration from blacks. He campaigned in the Negro community. He addressed black men and women as Mr., Miss, or Mrs., in defiance of an old southern custom that called for whites to speak to Negroes the way they spoke to children. Hartsfield was even photographed *shaking hands* with Negroes. That was unheard of in those days. But unlike most other white Atlantans, Hartsfield was paying attention to the tide of history. He knew that the days of the white primary were numbered. And in a city with the large Negro population that Atlanta had, a politician's appeal would soon have to be directed to all people in the city, regardless of skin color.

Except for Hartsfield, few whites seemed fully aware of what was ahead in Atlanta's political future. But in 1946, they all found out. During that year, the U.S. Supreme Court ruled, in the case of *Primus King* v. *The State of Georgia*, that the white primary was unconstitutional in depriving citizens of the right to vote on the basis of race. King, no relation to me, was a preacher from the town of Columbus, Georgia. He had worked with lawyers from the NAACP for several years as the case dragged through the lower courts. But he refused to give up, even in the face of threats to his life and actual attacks made upon him by whites.

Primus King's victory changed the South for every person living here, black or white. The immediate effect of the Supreme Court's decision was a doubling of the number of Negroes registered to vote in Atlanta, from 3,000 to nearly 6,800. The Atlanta Urban League conducted a registration drive under the direction of Grace Hamilton and Robert Thompson. By 1947, their efforts would place the names of 21,000 Negro voters on the rolls in Atlanta. Change now seemed to be in the very air we breathed. A new day had dawned. Bloc voting by Negroes would now have an effect on every politician, every campaign, and every political issue put before an enlarged constituency in Atlanta. Hartsfield had anticipated this, and he benefited handsomely. As mayor of the city, he would eventually hold office longer than anyone else in Atlanta's history.

The recurring dispute was over tactics: Should we try for negotiated settlements as opposed to divisive applications of political pressure? The difficulty that Negroes disposed to quiet counsel always ran into was that whites were often elusive and vague; they seemed to develop a lack of concentration almost as frequent as the common cold. To negotiate with whites meant coming to know that comment—I don't understand what you want—which was as regular as hello. When it came to under-standing what we wanted, whites in the church, in government, industry, in every walk of life, really, claimed ignorance more than any other defense. Negroes demanded to be treated like human beings, not pieces of property, and whites just stared, as if to say, How can you ask us to do this? Why change things, when we've been so happy with the way they've gone?

Very few whites in the South ever asked themselves to

account for what it cost to maintain their privileges. If any of them questioned what they had taken from others, or how much pain this taking caused, they kept peace with this awareness and never came forward to bear witness to their experience.

We pushed, but very gently by any modern standard, most of us accepting the premise that half a loaf was better than none, so long as the division was just temporary. What we were calling progress others saw as the end of a glorious way of life. We did not always take issue with that view so much as we tried to have whites—especially those who now had to campaign in districts with an increasingly large bloc of Negro voting precincts—urge the changes among their white constituents. After the League carefully checked a candidate's position on items of interest to Negro Atlantans, we would decide whether to endorse him. If we did, the endorsement would appear in Scott's newspaper, the *Daily World*, for as many voters as possible to see. But the major work of black leaders came in keeping the word alive, especially from our various pulpits and other forums, that voting was powerful as an agent of change. Registration drives never let up. Folks got bored, but the activity still went on throughout Negro Atlanta.

After the end of the Second World War, northern dollars began to be waved toward a developing South. In conversations with members of the League, Hartsfield often spoke of Atlanta as the nation's true city of the future. He walked a delicate line, though, hoping that in the long run everybody would benefit if he could keep encouraging the establishment of business ties with other parts of the country—especially the industrial North—while keeping a lid on some smoldering racial questions.

And while the effort on Hartsfield's part was never to be entirely successful while he was in office, very little progress in the city would have been made without him. The atmosphere he was instrumental in maintaining can be translated into statistical references that now seem antique. But the figures were anything but that when, in the year 1947, there were 24,000 registered black voters in Fulton County, Georgia, and 21,000 of them lived in Atlanta. These drives, directed by people like Grace Hamilton and Robert Thompson of the Urban

League, didn't resolve the racial crisis, but laid the ground-
work for all the possibilities of later civil-rights activity.

But no one should be left with the impression that we'd
found a way to control Atlanta politics; that just wasn't so. One
of the Negro community's great assets across America has been
the resistance to domination of the many by the few. We've
been a most democratic people throughout this nation's history,
sometimes to our own detriment—as when the majority oppresses
a minority through the law. But in Atlanta, during this period
around mid-century, there was never a day that passed when a
white person wouldn't just go to a few black leaders to order
our community around. As early as 1944, Benjamin Mays and
the other heads of the separate black colleges that comprised
the Atlanta University Complex formed the Southern Regional
Council to urge whites in power to bring down all forms of racial
discrimination. The group finally became integrated, but it was
bogged down constantly by resistance among the presumably
more enlightened members of the white leadership corps.
Eventually they just turned most of the work of dealing with
Negroes over to Mayor Hartsfield, who virtually had to dance
between the racial fortresses on both sides as mediator, inter-
preter, good guy, and architect of compromise.

One of the more pointed examples of this dance was Hartsfield's move to integrate the city police force in 1948. Caught
in a real tug-of-war over this issue, he eventually put blacks
in uniform, with full pay, but with power only to arrest other
blacks! As an indication of how many years have really passed
since that time, most blacks in Atlanta considered this a major
victory in the civil-rights struggle to that moment. I was one
who wasn't satisfied with the arrrangement, but I had few
allies this time. It was three years before Negro officers gained
full arrest powers in a strange police department that continued to fight skin color more than it fought crime—and would
do so for many more years. After a time, most Atlanta Urban
League members backed me on this fight for full arrest powers
for Negro cops, but some scars were left in the aftermath,
wounds that would never completely heal.

We particularly enjoyed a victory that came in 1947, after
eleven years of court sessions that dragged on and on for no

reason I could see, except our opposition's unwillingness to accept defeat gracefully. This was the fight for the equalization of teachers' pay scales without regard to race. The lawsuit, brought by Atlanta's black teachers with financial backing from Ebenezer, involved Mr. William H. Reeves, an Atlanta school-teacher, as the plaintiff. Mr. Samuel Davis, another teacher, was also a plaintiff. However, "Bill" Reeves was the principal and was dismissed from his job by the Atlanta Board of Education. But along with the teachers in the struggle, we had arranged with the Atlanta Life Insurance Company, a Negro institution, for them to hire Reeves as soon as the Atlanta Board of Education sent him a dismissal notice. We had to guarantee this job security before anyone would become involved with the court case.

And now, after more than a decade of humiliating delays, the black teachers had forced a change that made them equal before the law and their peers in the profession. The Federal District Court in Atlanta, ruling in our favor, said simply that paying a person less money because of the color of his skin just couldn't be.

The triumph was rich and made all of us glad. But it also reminded me once more that we'd not had the support of everyone in our own community on this one until the courts decided in our favor. Then the bandwagon suddenly became overcrowded with people who had told us, when we were recruiting help, "Well, no, I don't think I want to get involved in that stuff. . . . I've got them putting a lot of heat on me right now."

There had always been excuses. Someone's mortgage served as one kind of hammer to keep him away from controversy. Some others were tied into white interests in so many complicated ways that they felt extremely vulnerable. Those of us who could not be so easily threatened or pressured had to be the ones taking the stronger stand. I had to recall, however, one meeting at which every Negro minister in attendance told me that he wouldn't go with me to picket City Hall over the segregated water fountains and elevators. I told them that our unity on this issue was vital, because they'd be safe from arrest, at least, if there were a substantial number of us, too

many to toss into jail together. I ended up going alone, and
finally going inside City Hall to try to use several elevators on
both sides of the color line. As I thought I would be, I was
threatened with arrest. This was repeated several times until
the whole thing was more embarrassing to City Hall than it
was to me, so they took the signs out of the elevators. We
then set our sights on the fountains.

In 1914, a new site for Ebenezer was found, and the present
church building was completed shortly thereafter. The new
red brick structure on Auburn Avenue was a fine and solid
one, made to last, and located only a few blocks from Atlanta's
main black business district. Down the street, Negro commerce
had blossomed. A man named Hemon Perry had set the tone
long ago, forming the Standard Life Insurance Company back
in 1913. With this as a base, he tried to build an empire in the
service industries: dry cleaning, construction, drugstores, mort-
gage-loan companies, and land-development operations.

Hemon overextended himself, and his capital eventually dried
up; by 1924, it was all downhill for him. But he had established
a kind of legend along the avenue, which came to be known
as "Sweet Auburn." Other adventurous businessmen came after
him, and a few, learning from his errors, were able to sustain
their enterprises. By 1948, Atlanta Life Insurance, started back
in 1905 by a one time barber named Alonzo F. Herndon, had
assets close to $20 million. Banks opened, run by Negroes, and
run very well. C. A. Scott first put out the *Atlanta Daily World*
from his headquarters on Auburn.

All seemed well. . . .

At home, our children were growing up around us like three
impatient weeds, each one curving in a different direction.
Christine, quiet and extremely polite, was often teased by her
more rambunctious younger brothers. Alfred Daniel, A.D. to
all of us and to his friends, could get a little rough at times
and let his toughness build a reputation throughout our neighborhood. Martin Luther, Jr., was always a little sensitive in his
responses to even the most casual matters, and he was always
one to negotiate a dispute instead of losing his temper. Well,
nearly always. One summer afternoon when three youngsters

were playing around the house, A.D. was antagonizing his sister to the point where she was close to tears. It was all fun to him, but as Bunch and I sat out in the back yard we heard a yelp, and went inside to discover that the great little negotiator, M.L., had conked his battling brother over the head with a telephone, leaving him dazed and wobbly on his feet. Fortunately, we were all able to laugh—eventually—over this reversal of styles.

I'd begun thinking about the future of my youngsters, and in the rush to help them grow up a little faster than they wanted to—especially the boys—I began easing them toward a special attention to the ministry.

A.D. just backed away from this. He was a child who was determined from his earliest days not to be what his father was. At times he got so dramatic about it that we had a few run-ins over the matter, even while he was still very young.

For his part, M.L. said very little about preaching as his life's work, and—unreasonably, I guess—that made me believe through his earliest years that he would evolve more naturally than A.D. to a place in the pastorate of Ebenezer.

"Don't push the boys too hard, King," Bunch would often warn me. "It's easy to turn children away from things that *you* want so much. Let them be who they'll be."

Well, this was a difficulty. M.L., for instance, was a great speaker as a young boy, and he sang, too, in a fine, clear voice. His schoolwork, in both the private and public institutions he attended, was always of a high caliber. And he loved church, in a way I could recall in myself: the feeling for ceremonies and ritual, the passionate love of Baptist music.

I felt at times I was seeing much of myself in both the boys. A.D.'s angry response to being wronged, even slightly—I'd been there. I knew that they'd been spared some bruises of the spirit because they grew up in a relatively prosperous environment, bringing them little contact with the sort of naked bigotry of what was now, for me, "the old country." But they sensed things, both of them, that southern men must be aware of if they are black: the subtle moods and shifts of violent disposition, the low-burning flame of rage that never seems to go away in the Deep South.

I'd look at my children and remember again how much my father wanted me to farm when I was growing up. His life had been in those fields, along the rows of cotton and corn, in the woods where he hunted for food, or on land where he remained a stranger because the very ground he stood on always belonged to somebody else. I had seen a different road. Not wanting to live my father's life, I chose to walk in another direction. And yet, like him, I wanted so much to help my own boys shape *their* future. My daughter's life as an educator seemed a goal that her mother and I were duty-bound to help Christine achieve. But it was Bunch who regularly expressed the concern both of us felt in trying to understand where the parent ends and the child begins. I could not stand in their way, a very old, very human feeling. I loved the children too much to deny them anything, especially *themselves*, that sense all three of them developed in regard to who *they* wanted to be.

But I really saw the boys becoming ministers and Christine a teacher. It was in these areas that I knew I could help them. Our Baptist world of fellowship was built around family ties, school and fraternal relationships, the so-called hometown connections that kept phones ringing and letters moving in consideration of help requested and granted, favors offered and accepted. The world is too tough for anyone to think of challenging it alone. As a father, I wanted to be certain that my children went out into that world with skills to compete and self-respect to maintain themselves in all human encounters. I wanted them to have support from me to call on in achieving their goals. All of which sounded beautiful at the breakfast or dinner table. Only one thing worried me about it, though. The boys said right along they weren't going to be preachers!

Ten

By the late 1940s I was at that point in my own life where a man must begin thinking about how much he will live to see and how much he will be able to do before there is no more time for him to work. In the South of those years, the vision many of us had carried so far, a vision of full equality among Americans, was still more years away from fulfillment than it was comfortable to think about. Unless a major effort was made, the twentieth century would just drift into the twenty-first with the crippling disease of racism still very much an epidemic across this country.

In that frame of mind, I knew I had to reach out to my sons for their help in a matter of the greatest importance. For it was not just I who would need the vigor of a new generation's commitment to justice, but all of this country. Not only my sons were going to be needed in an ongoing, ever-difficult battle, but the sons of everybody in this nation who wanted to see America grow beyond what it had become. There was no draft for this army. A Civil War that had never really ended would now be fought on several fronts: moral, legal, social, and political. Wherever people worked or lived or went to school, there would be this great combat. The Negro could only struggle, there was no place to surrender to, no place where people could be spiritually alive. If anything was to give, it was going to have to be on the white side, where there was room to budge, and space to change.

I was beginning to feel that by repeating myself over and over on the issues that still affected the lives of Negro Americans, I was sounding like the proverbial broken record. But there could be no thought of stopping. A man grew older all the time, but he could never stop moving forward in his life. There was always so much to do, to learn, and to teach.

One day the two young sons of a local grocery-store owner told M.L. they couldn't play with him anymore. When he asked why, they said it was because they were white and he wasn't. This was about the time of the shoe-store incident, when the clerk had asked us to move to the back room in order to be waited on. That was just a store, but this was about friends, little fellows he played ball with, climbed trees with, guys he thought were true friends. Bunch was hardly able to console him. His heart, he said, was broken. How could anybody refuse to be a friend with somebody else because they were not the same color? "Why?" he asked his mother. "Why don't white people like us, Mother dear?"

Bunch sat and talked with him for hours. He was a curious youngster who really did wonder constantly about this peculiar world he saw all around him.

"Don't you be impressed by any of this prejudice you see," she told him. "And never think, son, that there is anything that makes a person *better* than you are, especially the color of his skin."

Bunch was very gifted with children. She raised all of ours with great love and respect for their feelings. I, on the other hand, had a temper. My impatience made it very hard for me to sit down with the boys and quietly explain to them the way I wanted things done. With M.L. and A.D., I found that a switch was usually quicker and more persuasive, although I never had to use this form of punishment with Christine. She was the exceptionally well-behaved, serious, and studious member of the trio.

Bunch insisted, though, as the children grew older, that any form of discipline used on them by either of us had to be agreed upon by both parents. This often curbed my temper, but it also helped Bunch to understand the things that made me angry. We talked a lot about the future of the kids, and she was able to understand that even when I got very upset with them, it was only because I wanted them to be strong and able and happy.

When the boys began earning a little money through neighborhood odd jobs, Bunch promoted a very simple plan for them. They were to consider the division into three parts of all the money their jobs or allowances brought them. Bunch called these divisions "the King home's three S's": Spending, Saving, and Sharing. In these and other ways, compared to the modern home environment, we ran a very tight ship. The children got to school on time every morning; they did homework as soon as they reached home in the afternoon, then chores. After supper, they did some studying, then we had prayers.

Bunch had grown up an only child, although her parents had raised other youngsters whose own parents were unable to care for them. She could be strict, in her way, and the kids learned early on that as gentle as their mother was, they couldn't get up early enough in the morning to fool her, any day of the week. She knew each of her children almost as well as she knew herself. M.L. came along with sensitivities only she could investigate and soothe. Bunch could also point out to me, when I couldn't see it, how much A.D. sounded like me when I was younger and she'd known me as a stubborn young country fellow trying to make up his own mind about where he was going.

I believed very strongly during this period of my life that to change Atlanta would be to change the entire South. And along with many others, I felt that this change would come more slowly than we wanted, but that counting on the basic human decency of all peoples was the best way to get anything accomplished if it involved fundamental changes in the way folks had lived most of their lives. From those nights in class at the Bryant School, when I'd first heard of government and elections and politicians and constituencies, the thought had remained with me that whatever Negroes accomplished in the South in my lifetime would have something to do with the ballot box. Year by year, I was convinced, we would work on the two fronts that eventually had to get us over: fighting to bring about an end to the white primary, which prevented our exercising a voice in local affairs involving our taxes and the fundamental human rights that were at the foundation of everything we fought for; and working in black communities to see that a maximum number of Negro voters were actually registered and ready to use that franchise to free our lives from the bonds of second- and third-class citizenship.

The ballot was the key. And the battle lines were drawn very clearly. Whites who were able to see the handwriting on the wall were already crying *Never!* even as our voices in the Negro community were preparing to sing out the new hymn of *Now!!*

I was active in the Atlanta Voters' League, a nonpartisan organization about evenly split in membership between Republicans and Democrats from the Negro community. Politically, I had seen value in both parties, and deficiencies as well. So I determined very early in my experience as a voter to support candidates instead of parties. I have in my life voted for Republican and Democratic presidential candidates and been supportive of those candidates without regard to party lines. This was my style in the Voters' League. Others disagreed. Franklin Roosevelt had impressed a lot of people in moving the country through the crisis of economic collapse and world war. I shared the enthusiasm that millions of Americans displayed for him. But I was also impressed by the support to southern Negro education that had been provided by the Rockefeller family. The Rockefellers were Republicans. I didn't believe in labels, so I found myself relating more and more to the complicated but wondrous American identity with its many variations and backgrounds.

The League was never taken over by any single political ideology. Freedom for all people was our goal, and we knew that in America that was going to mean working with everybody to whom this nation was important. We knew we had to begin a push toward a world where people did not have to live in constant fear because they were poor or the wrong color.

The lie that formed around southern life during this period was pushing us all toward an explosive confrontation over the racial question. Segregation had become an arrangement between whites and Negroes, a plan designed to hide the truth from both groups. Leadership on both sides moved further and further away from the masses of people who were most affected by the philosophy of separatism. Whites had placed the Negro leadership halfway between white complacency and black anger. Instead of working with us, whites wanted us merely to carry messages back to our people, saying that everything was all right in the segregated world, and only the Negroes who had no regard for Atlanta's or the nation's future would ever think about making trouble in paradise. But the trouble was already there, and the Negro hadn't been responsible for creating it in the first place. Now, in reacting against the system that dishonored everyone who lived comfortably within it, we became the troublemakers.

With a new militancy growing every day among black Americans all over the United States, and an increased amount of resistance on the part of whites to the aspirations of our people, the southern situation seemed to drift closer and closer to a chaotic upheaval. The coalition between whites in business and government and Negro leaders in the city, although functioning, was grinding slowly to a halt as far as any real movement toward social change was concerned. And this coalition had once been viewed as the true hope for the better life our city should have been able to enjoy.

Among the whites in leadership, I believe William Hartsfield may have been alone in his desire to make Atlanta into one city instead of two. The others just didn't seem to realize that unity was the only means of maintaining their power and achieving harmony. Dividing people by color was a practice living on borrowed time. White businessmen would often use those of us who'd been successful in the South as proof that separation of the races did really work to the benefit of both whites and blacks. White politicians tried over and over to convince Negro leaders that nothing was to be gained by mixing people together when they were doing just fine in their divided camps. And many Negroes who loved their city and this country tried for years to work out a reasonable solution to the grievances our people shared with us all the time. The more we pushed for a new day, however, the more complacent whites seemed to become, the more satisfied with the old ways. Just their indifference to the suffering of Negroes who weren't well off or basking in any limelight created a swelling of impatience. Our warnings to Hartsfield and the others that it was increasingly difficult to convince younger people to wait any longer for the rights their Constitution guaranteed them just weren't being heard. The storm kept brewing.

Very severe differences of opinion split two generations of black Atlanta and most of the other black communities across the United States following the end of the Second World War. Black men serving in the armed forces returned to the South with a world view, having seen Europe and the Far East, and knowing clearly how the lie of racial segregation was being spread all over the earth. They were eager and unafraid. Those of us who were older responded to the South more patiently, perhaps, because we had seen it even worse in earlier times. Our timetables, that of the younger and that of the more experienced, were decidedly different. Blacks established in careers and homes may not have been so enthusiastic about direct action, certainly not at the beginning of the sit-ins and other demonstrations. But folks did change. Some of them lost what they could never recover, but they moved with the times and followed young dynamic leaders along the road toward a new day.

At first things moved slowly. There had always been the impatient and the hot-tempered in the community, but they generally could be calmed down to the point where more reasonable voices prevailed. I had spoken out of turn at meetings of the Voters' League on one or two occasions. Nothing serious—small differences in viewpoint and approach. But the black coalition had been large enough to contain my rough edges and the smoother, less abrasive style of the famed Atlanta activist John Wesley Dobbs. Now the entire coalition process was under challenge. The kids no longer believed in anything we stood for, or so the talk was going. They'd lost confidence, and it would soon be too late to mend all the bridges that had been breaking down right in front of us, for so many years.

The battles of the Negro middle class had separated from those of the poor, and the groups seemed to be drifting in different directions within the same struggle for human dignity and constitutional rights.

The matter entered my home in 1950. My daughter, Christine, had been graduated from Spelman and had continued her studies at Columbia University Teachers College in New York City. I was pleased with her determined pursuit of knowledge, although I should have realized it couldn't just go on forever. She was a somewhat shy young woman who had, of course, confided in her mother that she was interested in the teaching profession, but she had said nothing to me. In this she was much the same as her brothers, who never wanted me to use any influence on their behalf. I spoke often with the mayor, the chief of police, the head of the Atlanta Board of Education; this is what the coalition had always been about—a spirit of communication between leaders on both sides of a racial fence.

The hard part was getting into the general public arena the harmony we were usually able to bring to those meetings. I was able, for instance, to help my daughter to be hired as a teacher in Atlanta—when it had been determined earlier that she would never get such a job. I was still identified in town as the leader of those dangerous radicals from way back in 1936, who'd battled eleven years to equalize teacher salaries, forcing white teachers to live on the same rates of pay blacks worked for. And so Christine was being punished for the "sins" of her father.

I had been busy with the business of the world and had not even noticed Christine's intense desire to teach. And so I hadn't seen that the forces locked against her in a most evil way were the same ones mounting the resistance to every part of our struggle. To confront what they had done to my child in getting back at me was to come face-to-face with the tasks of tomorrow. Bunch tried all of one afternoon to calm me down when I discovered what had happened. "Why didn't she tell me she wanted to teach?" I was shouting around the house. "Because," Bunch answered, "she believes in merit, King, just as you and I have taught her to believe in it, and she doesn't want a job

just because she happened to be born your daughter. She could
spend the rest of her life being told she didn't have a brain in
her head, that she was working only because you pulled some
strings. . . ."

Christine had taken two master's programs following her
graduation from Spelman College. When she received her first
master's, she applied for a teaching position with the Atlanta
Board of Education. Her request was denied, and she returned
to Columbia for a second master's. She again applied to the
Atlanta Board of Education, and again her request was denied.
Now, my daughter was so well qualified that the school system
should have been begging her to come to work.

I was busy being proud of her and wrestling with the demon
South, and I had missed the center of all this. M.L. and his
mother often mentioned that Christine had earned one master's
in 1949, and would have another one in a year or so, and
wouldn't it be fine if she stayed right here in town and taught
school? Years later they'd remind me of how often I had nodded,
"Yes, yes," and "Sure, sure," to their conversation, remembering
the sound but not always the words.

Finally Christine brought it to me directly. A woman named
Miss Bazoline Usher, who was chief supervisor of Negro teachers
for the school system, came to our home to share with us information that so disturbed her that she risked losing her job to tell
us about it. Christine's applications were being routinely filed
away, never to be seriously considered. She would never teach
in Atlanta.

I called the mayor. We talked for a while about raising children, and then we moved over to how he felt about political
opponents who took things out on each other's families. He
assured me that nothing like that would be tolerated in his
administration. So I told him about my daughter's job search
and her difficulties in being placed in the school system, and I
reminded him of the long teacher equalization fight that got
so bitter in and out of court over those many years. And the
mayor listened quietly. He then told me to expect a call from
him within the half hour, and asked if I'd have my daughter on
the phone when he called back. Several minutes later, he

called to tell an elated Christine that Miss Ira Jarrell, superintendent of the Atlanta schools, would personally be welcoming her to a teaching position at the W. H. Crogman School, in the Pittsburgh section of the city, along with all of her new peers in education who'd be gathering in just a few days to begin a new school term.

Now I realized, in a more personal way than ever before, just how limited this kind of coalition politics had become when so much could be done through a phone call to the mayor, but so little ever came out of meetings between Negro leaders and whites in the power structure when it came to issues affecting everyone in the city. The power of the black sector of the coalition rested more on an ability to get a favor done now and then rather than on any real political clout. Negroes could advise, or even irritate, like a tight shirt collar that rubs the skin sore if it's worn long enough. But this wouldn't do. Power —not just favors and good deeds now and then—had to be shared among all people if social change were ever to become a reality in Atlanta. This required mutual respect and a healthy regard for the principles of democracy America told the world we practiced without prejudice toward anyone. Favors were now seen by young black people as more evidence that Atlanta's more fortunate Negroes had a special deal going with whites that excluded the black masses in favor of a black elite. The poor had to ride segregated buses and trains. Others had fine cars to get around in. The poor had to use substandard public rest rooms, and they were forced to accept inferior school facilities. Others avoided these things, often through private education for their children. Such people could refuse to challenge laws that discriminated against those who could not afford, economically, to get around them. Meanwhile, members of the coalition seemed to be saying more and more that patience was the answer, a dialogue was continuing and would soon produce results.

All that *sounded* fine and fancy, younger people were beginning to repeat, but what does it accomplish, this coalition? How can grown men sit in a room at City Hall and look across a table at one another, get up later and congratulate each other on doing such good work toward progress, when people couldn't use the same drinking fountain in a city park if they were different colors?

We were running out of time. The excuses had been used up. People wanted answers that made sense for a country surging through the most technologically advanced period in history, when disease was being conquered, when the machinery in our lives gave us travel and enormous comfort in all our working and social lives. We could speak to people thousands of miles away on the telephone but not a seat away on a city bus. A Negro could feed a white child, virtually live in a white home day by day, and still be considered unfit to be spoken to in a public place. And for the Negro who both aspired to more and achieved it, the emphasis placed on skin color throughout the South changed only slightly on the way up any social ladder black folks could pursue.

The experience with Christine would provide much of the seed of thought for a sermon I regularly delivered in one form or another over the years, built around the premise of "Misplaced Emphasis." You see, I would tell the Ebenezer congregation, important things can be lost although they are right before you, because of misplaced emphasis. You may think that all the meetings, and the picketing, and the marches are the center of your life . . . only to discover that you have misplaced your emphasis if the very core of the reason that you meet and march and picket and protest is so near you can reach out and touch it easily, not realizing that it was, in fact, so close. You say sometimes that you must look at the larger picture because this is where all the answers are bound to be . . . and you find out that maybe they aren't there at all, that again you have misplaced your emphasis, and you've got to look even closer to yourself to see what is really there. And this same misplaced emphasis occurs (are you listening?) when you think that everything is going well because your car drives so smoothly, and your new suit fits you so well, and those high-priced shoes you bought make your feet feel so good; and you begin to believe that these things, these many luxuries all around, are the really important matters of your life. Then you have misplaced your emphasis *again* and failed to see truth pulling at your sleeve . . . say it's tuggin' at you, wants to get closer. Truth wants to come right up and say, Don't misplace that emphasis anymore—put it in the right place! And see where the real matter lies. . . .

At Voters' League meetings I found myself doing more shouting than I'd ever done anywhere before in my life. My voice often came rolling out in the preacher's cadence to see who else felt we weren't asking for enough. However we asked for it, we had to push harder, for more, and sooner.

Even as the young people of Atlanta clearly saw us as part of the problem, we began to see their shift in attitude as one that created division constantly. To them, this was the point. You can't leave us behind, they were saying. We're your children, we're in front of you. But if the past is where you want to stay, or have to, then we will leave you there and move on.

Perhaps it was a sign of the impatience that was coming that M.L. decided to skip his final year at Washington High School and enter Morehouse College as a fifteen-year-old freshman. In a way both distant and close to my decision at that age to go off and become rich working on the railroad, my son had decided to reach higher. The risk for millions of people, of course, is that in doing this, their grip fails, they fall back and never quite get going again; yet millions more follow in those footsteps. My pride swelled, though, because M.L.'s confidence simply left no room in our house for uncertainty. He was going to take the step that told him what nothing else could: where he was going. Bunch, though she was enthusiastic, also recognized that my great joy over M.L.'s decision had a lot to do with knowing that by enrolling at Morehouse, he chose to be in Atlanta, near the daily influence of a father who still had no co-pastor at his church. Of course, if a young man couldn't be convinced in four years . . .

Eleven

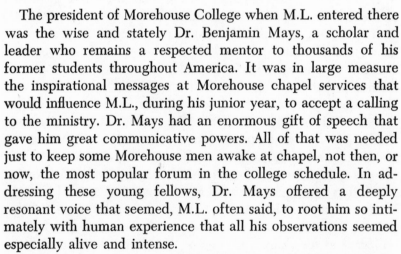

The president of Morehouse College when M.L. entered there was the wise and stately Dr. Benjamin Mays, a scholar and leader who remains a respected mentor to thousands of his former students throughout America. It was in large measure the inspirational messages at Morehouse chapel services that would influence M.L., during his junior year, to accept a calling to the ministry. Dr. Mays had an enormous gift of speech that gave him great communicative powers. All of that was needed just to keep some Morehouse men awake at chapel, not then, or now, the most popular forum in the college schedule. In addressing these young fellows, Dr. Mays offered a deeply resonant voice that seemed, M.L. often said, to root him so intimately with human experience that all his observations seemed especially alive and intense.

And of course this reminded me of my student days and the sound of those legendary Morehouse voices that seemed to thunder information through any wall of resistance: C. D. Hubert, Dean of the School of Religion, whose three hundred or so pounds had always given his lectures a special kind of solidity. Dr. Hubert was named Acting President of Morehouse

College, succeeding Dr. Samuel Howard Archer, who was an outstanding scholar and a tough, athletic sort of man, who we all felt could have instilled pride in a pebble by the roadside. Their call was for hard work and high achievement. The faculty had always been dedicated to turning out yearly graduating classes of men who considered being Morehouse graduates something especially distinguished.

During M.L.'s years there, George Kelsey, in the theology department, saw the pulpit as a place both for drama, in the old-fashioned, country Baptist sense, and for the articulation of philosophies that address the problems of society. And Dr. Mays, an elegant speaker, offered the tempering of that drama with calm assurance and unassailable reason. M.L. was clearly impressed by those first three years, and told his mother one evening that he would enter the ministry. After sharing the news with me, M.L. agreed to a trial sermon at Ebenezer, where he found a crowd waiting to bear witness, a crowd that grew so rapidly on a Sunday afternoon that we had to move him into the main sanctuary so he could finish. M.L. had found himself. I could only thank God, pretty regularly, for letting me stay around long enough to be there.

Oddly enough, we had a fairly heated argument shortly thereafter. For weeks he'd been telling me about some meetings at Morehouse and some of the other schools, and the formation of a group called the Intercollegiate Council. I thought little of what sounded to me like an ordinary student organization, until he told me that it was integrated. White students had joined, and mixed meetings were now taking place on the white campuses and the Negro campuses, under the guiding spirit of Mrs. Dorothy Lilley, a white Methodist woman.

"I don't like it, M.L.," I said to him. "You don't need to risk any betrayals from them, and that's mainly what you'll get. . . ."

He answered that he had to take that risk, and he remained in the group, explaining when again I asked him to quit: "Dad, I know I could resent every person in the white race, and it would be easy. That's the point. It would be too easy, and I know the answer to so much of this is more complicated."

He spoke of the fundamental decency of whites that could never be overlooked as we struggled for our own rights as full citizens and human beings in this country. To forget, he added, was simply to become the very people we've been fighting against. . . . He had learned, M.L. told me, that we had to act morally, no matter whom or what we were fighting.

He was quick to remind me, too, that my own comments about men like William Hartsfield had given him a sense that we could—we had to—look for allies among those whites who understood and those who would learn, even as we were learning, how much this great country could do for itself. "There is time, Dad," he explained further. "I know we have time if we build from among all the groups we can depend on and trust. And I know they're out there!"

He was much more certain than I was. In my mind there were recollections of how many times the white ministry, for example, might have done exactly what M.L. was telling me about now. Each time one move was made, by an individual expecting to be supported by others, others moved to push the races even further apart. And those pushing seemed so much more successful than those who tried to pull people together. "We've got to work with them," I told M.L., "God knows this. But be careful about these meetings, this willingness to trust those who can be friends or enemies from one day to the next."

But M.L. had made his point quite well, and had given his stubborn old father new food for thought. Even in my desire to make him a little more cautious, I'd run out of arguments. America was approaching the middle of a century where change was constant, and those who could not change soon were distanced by the rest of any society. How far had I thought the South would continue with segregation as a way of life? Years? Centuries? Nothing was going to bring us a new day unless it included the very simple, often overlooked communication between races as partners rather than adversaries. What M.L. had found in his Intercollegiate Council went on constantly in the meetings held between the Voters' League members and Atlanta city officials: an attempt to find resolutions.

The atmosphere at Morehouse created in its students a desire for excellence. M.L. saw this as meaning much more than gifted scholarship. And he saw his undergraduate studies as one step among several that would take him closer to an understanding not only of the particulars of the human condition, but of what could be done about them. It was not enough just to acquire an education because it was available. He was finding that not all of his classmates considered their pursuit of a degree in terms of values beyond finding a job.

"Dad," M.L. said to me one day, "Herman Talmadge has a Phi Beta Kappa key, can you believe that? What did he use all that precious knowledge for? To accomplish what?" Talmadge had been governor of Georgia for too long a time, and he came from a long line of segregationist politicians who appealed to voters by feeding their hatred of Negroes.

"The most dangerous criminal," M.L. wrote in a student paper during his senior year at Morehouse, "may be the man gifted with reason, but with no morals."

A.D. was experiencing a period of crisis in his life. He entered then dropped out of Morehouse, convinced that he could never be a minister. We argued, mainly over his dropping out of school, which I thought he should continue whether he chose to preach or not. I knew the pressure had bothered him, the constant comparisons to his brother, the great success Christine had maintained with her scholarship and, not the least of it, my stubborn insistence that he could do anything I wanted him to.

He went out and got himself a job selling insurance, and he did this without asking me for help through my contacts in the city's business community. In a way I liked his doing it that way, though Bunch would remind me for years afterward how annoyed I'd been when I found out.

My worries about A.D. increased in another area, however, when he began to talk a lot about getting married, settling down, and raising his own family. Nothing would make him any more independent in my eyes, we both knew that. I was praying he wouldn't take such a step before giving his education another chance. But the more the subject came up between us, the more clear it became that he was talking about being in love. The time for infatuation was over very early with A.D. He was not dating several young women or going out a lot to social affairs. His moods were focused on the serious side of home life.

Bunch didn't have to tell me, although I acted like I didn't really know, that at age twenty my younger son had made up his mind that what *he* wanted for his life would have to be paid considerably more attention by everyone in his family. He wanted to be a husband and a father. His brother and sister were doing exceptionally well in school. A.D. wasn't as interested in school as the two of them, and he knew this sooner than the rest of us admitted it. On June 17, 1950, he married Naomi Barber, a gracious, warm young woman from Dothan, Alabama, who had grown up in Atlanta and was attending Spelman College. I had asked him to wait. He decided not to. And so we welcomed into our family its newest member. And we began that glorious wait for the child A.D. and Naomi were soon expecting, the grandchild, another generation to remind us all of time moving with or without notice, and life continuing as gently and quietly as it always had.

The years would prove that A.D. was right in his choice of Naomi. They loved each other deeply, and in her quiet, unassuming manner she always gave him her full support as he completed his education, entered the ministry, and worked with his brother in the Movement. She balanced his robust, extroverted temperament because she was not easily ruffled. She has been a wonderful mother for their five children, displaying extraordinary calmness and courage since A.D.'s death, as an only parent.

I didn't oppose M.L.'s wish to continue his education with advanced graduate work after he'd received a degree from Morehouse in 1948, but my hope was that he'd soon join me as co-pastor at Ebenezer. He was a fine preacher. His voice, his delivery, the structure and design of his sermons all set him apart from anyone I'd ever heard in my life. And while I wasn't thinking about retiring just yet, slowing down some in the work of the ministry did enter my mind now and then. But when M.L. shared, first with his mother and Christine, then with A.D., and finally with me, his desire to continue formal studies in theology, we all encouraged him to pursue his own dreams. And so he went north to study, first at Crozer Seminary, in Pennsylvania, and later at Boston University. In both places he was able to broaden his knowledge tremendously, and he matured, as well, in both his personal and vocational life.

Bunch and I worried about the effect the northern social environment might have on him when he returned home. We remembered a summer when the boys had persuaded us to let them work in the tobacco fields up in Connecticut. They came back buzzing with stories about the integrated life of the North, and how different for the Negro such an existence was. They'd seen what they considered a freer society, and I don't think either of them was ever able to look at segregation afterward without burning with a determination to destroy that system forever. They were just young boys at this time, high-school students. But that summer they spent in Connecticut changed both of them a great deal. The North wasn't entirely without racial discord, of course, but there was some relief from the presence of laws intended to turn people into *things* that were less than human.

So, many of the young went north to school and never came back. This was a loss that hurt the South, perhaps for longer than anyone knows. Sons and daughters who loved the South, despite its failures, were driven away by the fury of the segregationist mind and heart. The South was always the part of America where the deepest emotions seemed to have been gathered for some special purpose. The task of making two people into one people in the same country was a matter for those with a strong will and a great resolve. And we came to a time when Americans had to find out whether we had the stuff to win an especially hard fight.

Coalition politics received a stiff challenge from a more radical sector of black Atlanta at precisely those points where it was most vulnerable. In a time when the speed of all other events was increasing, the snail's pace of southern politics made this region of the country seem as backward as some people liked to say it was, people who saw the signs and the dividing lines and the separated facilities and probably wondered how a city like Atlanta could call itself civilized when its opera house maintained a COLORED ENTRANCE.

Atlanta's reputation as the South's capital was built very

carefully over a period of many years. The Civil War had left a city of ashes. In earlier times, Atlanta had become a central point of the railroads as they crossed this area going west and north. As a terminal for the movement of freight to other parts of the United States, Atlanta became a stronghold for business, and a strong class of merchants and later industrialists formed here. Money made the area into a solid base for enterprising and hard-working southerners and people who were transplanted here, mainly to do business of one sort or another. Atlanta probably recovered from the War Between the States faster than any other city, North or South. People who came to the city wanted to build something special, something that would set them apart from any other part of the South. There were the merchant and the tradesman to dislodge the old landowning, slaveholding folks, who couldn't hang on to any of that and were finally pushed out by those who saw a model kind of city that could rival any other in the world.

All of this helped create the political climate of Atlanta as one that consistently favored the interests of businessmen. What was good for business was deemed to be perfect for the rest of the city, and there really could not be any departure from this philosophy that received serious attention, let alone political support. Politicians were traditionally the "friends" of the corporate mind here, and Atlanta's ties to the people often came after businesses had tied *their* knots with elected officials. So things could go slowly while business claimed that everything was fine because that's what the profit ledgers were showing. The illusion became real, and people took to fooling themselves easily until they lived day to day in a complete fantasy world.

As Hartsfield continued the work of bringing hundreds of industrial firms into Atlanta, the city seemed to boom. By the middle 1950s he would gain for this area the South's principal airport, probably the greatest single attraction for people looking to place any kind of major investment in the future of the South.

A lot of these efforts were extremely important economically, but they also managed to keep Atlanta isolated from some of the cities around it. It can be said that the Civil Rights Movement reached this city last because people here had been seeing

the developing rifts between whites and blacks through proverbial rose-colored glasses. The ripple going through much
of the South when the Supreme Court struck down segregation
in schools in 1954 wasn't received as passionately here—nothing
was during that period—and so the entire pattern of social
change moving through Atlanta seemed casual at times. As
progressive as the city was considered, its pioneer spirit seldom
extended past the walls of board rooms. Keeping things quiet
became an act and an art.

Being proud of a child is no risk, only a great pleasure. M.L.
was moving forward into a modern, advanced sort of ministry
requiring lengthy and dedicated study. I admired his mind's
receptivity and the genuine passion he had for learning. His
arguments, theological or not, were precisely constructed and
convincing. Politically, he often seemed to be drifting away
from the basics of capitalism and Western democracy that I
felt very strongly about. There were some sharp exchanges; I
may even have raised my voice a few times. But mainly it was
a rich period in my life, when a great wealth of knowledge
from around the globe could be imparted by a son to his
father. Listening to the fine sermons that combined so many
of the Bible's truths with wisdom of the modern world, I
marveled at how all was interwoven into a most compelling,
stirring oratory. M.L. was still a son of the Baptist South, there'd
never be any doubt about that. But there was a deeper, considerably more resonant quality in his preaching, and on the
Sundays he relieved me in the pulpit, I grew increasingly more
moved by his growth, the probing quality of his mind, the
urgency, the fire that makes for brilliance in every theological
setting.

My pride swelled even further when I spoke, by telephone,
with an old friend, the Reverend William H. Hester, pastor of
the Twelfth Street Baptist Church up in the Roxbury section of
Boston, who told me how impressed he'd been when M.L.
preached there for Sunday services on a couple of occasions.
In the company each time, Hester managed to add, of an
extremely attractive young lady.

Bunch was the first to notice that M.L. had stopped calling

home as much as he had when he'd first gone up to Boston to study. And I was the first to think that one of two things was possible when a young man in school lost interest in reversing the charges to telephone his parents, often for hours at a time, three or four times a week: the young man had been working too much, or he'd been partying too hard. Either way, he could be headed for trouble.

Now, as it happened, I'd been elected to the Morehouse Board of Trustees, and their annual meeting was being held in New York at about the time I became convinced my son was either in love or being driven into depression over the vast amounts of scholarly work he was now doing. School had never thrown M.L. before. But Bunch reminded me that M.L. had been getting pretty serious about a young lady in Atlanta. An engagement had been discussed. However, she wasn't hearing from him too regularly since he'd gone off to get his doctorate. Something was up. I decided to find out just what it was. Who, I wondered, was this attractive woman the Hesters talked about?

And so, during that winter of 1951, Bunch and I traveled to Boston following the Morehouse Trustees' meeting in New York and dropped in on M.L. at the apartment he shared in the Roxbury section with a young fellow, Philip Leund, who'd also graduated from Morehouse. They were both glad to see us, and Bunch congratulated them on the neat way in which they kept the apartment. I noticed that, too, but I wasn't so sure that these two fellows were responsible for the touches of housework so evident throughout the place.

Philip graciously volunteered to drive Bunch over to visit the Hesters, and M.L. and I settled down for a little talk. I could see immediately that I'd guessed correctly. The young man was so much in love, stars were just glittering in his eyes. But he sidestepped the issue when I brought it up. Later, I found out why. He didn't want to talk about Coretta Scott, he wanted to see her, and he wanted me to meet the young lady. She stopped by the apartment just a few minutes after Bunch and Phil Leund had left.

Coretta was a beautiful young woman from Marion, Alabama,

who'd been a student at Antioch College in Ohio before coming to Boston to study voice at The New England Conservatory of Music. She came from among strong, solid, courageous black folks who'd worked the land and built up businesses for themselves. Proud people who had produced, in Coretta, a fine, strong young daughter to carry on their traditions of hard work and high regard for education. From the moment she arrived, I knew M.L. was very much in love with her. Well, this worried me a bit. I knew of situations where young people hadn't been able to control their desire for one another and fell victims to their mutual affection instead of becoming beneficiaries of it. Coretta seemed extremely level-headed and serious. But as I watched them make eyes at each other across the room, they seemed even younger and less mature than I knew they were.

Bunch and I stayed in Boston for a few days, visiting with our friends the Hesters and seeing the city. M.L. and Coretta seemed to spend so much time together that I wondered when either of them got any studying done. And so on the afternoon Bunch and I planned to return to Atlanta, I decided to have a talk with the young lovers. Bunch had met Coretta only briefly and though their exchanges were very cordial, I didn't have the impression that they'd really hit it off too well. Still, we thought it would be a good idea to see each other for a half hour or so before Bunch and I caught our train. But as we sat in the living room of M.L. and Phil's apartment, it was very clear that my son and Miss Scott only had eyes for each other. Bunch sort of nodded at me during one point in the conversation about the weather, then asked Philip and M.L. to join her for a moment in the kitchen.

Coretta and I sat and talked together for several minutes before anything was really said. She was planning a career on the concert stage, which I hardly thought was appropriate for a young woman seeing a young man from a strict Baptist up-- bringing and background. Perhaps, I suggested, she'd find much more in common with someone from her own field of interest, music.

Coretta didn't let my words slip by her unnoticed, but she remained unruffled by them. I then hinted that both she and

M.L. were just experiencing a little infatuation that probably wouldn't last out the school term. She smiled but didn't fall for that bait, either.

Well, I got a bit tired of the fencing, and I spoke very bluntly to Coretta.

"Let me ask you very directly," I said. "Do you take my son seriously, Coretta?" She thought I was joking with her, because M.L. had been displaying his dry sense of humor most of the afternoon. In answer to my question, Coretta answered, rather cheerfully I thought, "Why, no, Reverend King, not really."

I felt myself turn warm under the collar. I was too angry to say anything right away, but as M.L. rejoined us, I found myself speaking very rapidly to Coretta. I told her I was glad she had no serious intentions as far as M.L. was concerned. Well, naturally, upon hearing this, M.L.'s jaw dropped almost to his belt buckle. I went right on telling Coretta I thought that, under the circumstances, M.L.'s mother and I would be just as happy if things were put right out in front, openly and honestly. . . .

Then, as people who speak a lot often will, I went a little too far, mentioning names, women to whom M.L. had proposed marriage.

She was very cool through all of this, and I told myself that Coretta Scott was nobody to try to intimidate with rhetoric. But stubbornly, with that old country mule rising up in me, I just went right on. "M.L.," I said, none too subtly, "has gone out with the daughters of some fine, solid Atlanta families, folks we've known for many years, people we respect, and whose feelings we'd never trample on. I'm talking, Coretta, about people who have much to share and much to offer."

She stood up. Anger flashed briefly through her eyes, but I could see also that Coretta Scott was determined not to lose control of herself. Her voice was very full and confident when she spoke.

"I have something to offer, Reverend King." And she made it crystal clear that she wasn't a giggly little girl with no substance or sense or spirit. She knew just what was at stake in her relationship with M.L. She would be able to see, just as I could, the looks of concern in the faces of Ebenezer's congregation on any Sunday morning when word got out that M.L. was becoming very serious about a woman who planned to be a musical artist. Would she continue with that, possibly traveling around the country to appear before cheering audiences and building up a following of adoring fans who left her almost no time for any personal life? Or would she just abandon that in favor of being the wife of a very promising young southern minister, mother to his children, a vital part of a tight-knit church community set very much in its own ways, which didn't include concert singing for the pastor's wife? These were difficult matters. Bunch understood very clearly the sacrifice many women had to make for their husbands in the ministry. She herself had been forced to give up a life in the educational system because she chose marriage over the work she'd been trained for. And now Coretta was facing the same kind of decision, with a quiet dignity that I couldn't help admiring. I still wasn't certain I wanted her to marry M.L., but I knew she was a person of substance.

M.L.'s mind, of course, was already made up. We went off to his room after I'd spoken with Coretta. He told me he wanted to marry her. I could still hear the fire in her voice as she told me, I have something to offer! And I knew that it was real between them, that no amount of discouragement was going to mean anything at all. And so I reluctantly agreed that perhaps they should marry, before anything happened that would force them to rush into a wedding that would bring a lot of embarrassed whispering to the ceremony.

"I must marry Coretta," said M.L. "She's the most important person to come into my life, Dad. I know you don't really approve, but this is what I have to do."

We returned to find that Bunch had gone downstairs with Philip and had him honking the horn of his car to get me started for the trip to the train station. I spoke briefly with Coretta before I left, just to assure her that I was not entirely pleased with what was going on between her and M.L., but that if he was convinced, I was sure that eventually I would be. And, eventually, I was. When they married, on the lawn of her parents' home in Marion, Alabama, on June 18, 1953, I pronounced them man and wife.

Twelve

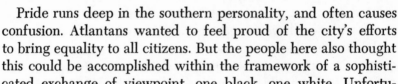

Pride runs deep in the southern personality, and often causes confusion. Atlantans wanted to feel proud of the city's efforts to bring equality to all citizens. But the people here also thought this could be accomplished within the framework of a sophisticated exchange of viewpoint, one black, one white. Unfortunately, racial discrimination was too primitive for this kind of process to continue indefinitely. And so while coalition politics ground slowly to a halt in Atlanta, another city in the South became the focal point of that period of history.

Montgomery, Alabama, had no coalition politics because whites there just couldn't bear the thought of communicating with any black people on such a level. In 1954, following the completion of his course work at Boston University, M.L. took the pastorate of Dexter Avenue Baptist Church in Montgomery. Within a year after he and Coretta had moved to the city, Rosa Parks set into motion America's most famous boycott. When she refused to give up her seat to a white passenger on a city bus, Mrs. Parks was arrested. Negroes responded with a boycott of the transit company that eventually bankrupted the bus lines. The famed Montgomery Bus Boycott was led by the Reverend

Martin Luther King, Jr. And although I'd been uneasy about the role he played in the beginning of this enormous national drama, I soon realized that the effort made in Montgomery *created* the Civil Rights Movement, and made all the other parts of it possible.

M.L. told me that Montgomery happened the way it did because the people there simply had no other choice but to participate in direct action to break the law in order to change it. The people in Alabama lived in what often came close to a police state as far as racial matters were concerned. Among the whites there were no voices of reason, no one willing to listen to the song of progress.

Atlanta had been inching along with the integration of city golf courses, which few Negroes used, and other small concessions designed to unravel slowly the pattern of segregated life. And all the things that were accomplished in Montgomery would eventually have come about in Atlanta and other parts of the South, but not before many years had passed. Montgomery changed the concept of time as it relates to social change. The boycott there also made it clear that segregation was an economic matter, not merely a political one. When the pressure of profits being lost is felt in this society, all things begin turning very quickly. Those who do not change, fall. The bus company in Montgomery held on stubbornly to a policy of segregated seating long after there was nothing but the vanity of white supremacists left at stake. By then it was too late, and the bus line was destroyed, swept away by new time. When the Supreme Court of the United States held that separate seating in a public vehicle, because of race or color, was unconstitutional, a great victory had been won. Yet Montgomery stood virtually alone in its boycott effort.

I was still in favor of boycotts, which I will always feel are the greatest weapon possessed by any disadvantaged people. But some people in Atlanta, including many blacks, remained uncertain about marching or demonstrating. There were Negroes who were embarrassed by the thought of making a public display of any concern they had, no matter how deep. And whites took advantage of this attitude. As long as the system of segregation was a matter for discussion, blacks were caught in a trap.

Southern white folks are among the greatest talkers and story-tellers in the world. They can go on for hours, for days and weeks, just running their mouths without ever getting tired. Without a tactic to break that flow of talk, nothing would ever have been solved for the Negro in the South during the middle of this century. A boycott brought all the chatter to a halt. White businessmen feared boycotts more than they feared the flood. You could get insurance against the rising waters, but nobody paid off for stores that shut down because a bunch of "niggers" decided to stop spending what little money they had with people who didn't consider them human.

Atlanta didn't want to push. The golf courses were integrated during this time because a Negro boycott of the municipal golf links would have had no effect. Only a handful of blacks in the city were golfers. Thousands rode the buses. Consequently, not much more than a half-dozen people were on hand that morning in the summer of 1955 when Hartsfield resisted pressure to close the golf courses rather than integrate them. First he had had racist remarks painted off the benches and buildings around the links, and had warned parks department employees that insulting Negroes who used golf courses would be grounds for dismissal from their jobs.

But a couple of years after the golf-course integration, it became clear that this tactic was going to have a shorter life than many people expected. During the summer of 1957, the president of Atlanta Transit, Robert Sommerville, began holding regular meetings with Hartsfield and several of us from the Negro community. The matter we discussed was the orderly transition to an integrated bus system. Once again, the Atlanta Plan was to be followed: one nonviolent action, arrests, and subsequent integration through court decree. I maintain to this day that there was nothing basically wrong with this approach, except that it took too long and never got to the roots of segregation, those deeper places in the human soul where the law did not reach. If America was going to become one country instead of two, more than seats on buses would have to be shared. But I was also growing weary of complaints about what a *character* I was becoming for seeking firmer, more direct types of action against the institutions that promoted racism in the country. I had learned from Montgomery—where the action, direct or not, had required so long to complete—that the long pent-up *feelings* about segregation were emotional time bombs that had to be defused rather than hidden even further away. The South had to come out of a very old shell and look at itself, honestly, and with the courage to face up to what it had been. That couldn't be accomplished through polite ceremonies alone. For all the passion that was ignited in Alabama, people seemed relieved that so much of the tension could be released, so much fear among whites and blacks could be overcome. In Atlanta, everything would be done with smiles and handshakes, the way it's done when monuments are dedicated, or ships are sent off to sea with the smashing of a bottle of champagne.

Sommerville was a very convincing speaker. He quoted the findings of a study commissioned by the local bus company in conjunction with several black Atlanta civil-rights organizations. Negro passengers had a case that could be taken to court. The bus company was willing to lose in court—that was a gentleman's way of losing, after all. No white businessman could put up with losing directly to the Negro. The courts could instruct them, not black folks. And of course there was a lot of publicity value to get out of all this, too. BUS COMPANY OBEYS LAW; that sort of thing.

The Reverend William Holmes Borders, pastor of the Wheat Street Baptist Church, liked the idea of the court case resolving the bus-segregation struggle, and he agreed to support it. This would be a very visible kind of evidence for the young people, he argued; they'd now see something concrete that coalition politics had achieved; the value of cooperation between antagonists would be stressed.

There were others in the black community who felt that the results of the study pointed out the new power Negroes possessed in the southern political firmament. Fifty-three percent of Atlanta's bus passengers, the study revealed, were black. The loss of their business would be dangerous. Negroes, the study really pointed out, no longer had to *ask* for anything.

Sommerville probably recognized this as clearly as anyone. He offered promises, for example, that Negroes would find jobs that had never been open to them before within the framework of the Atlanta transportation system, and that even more blacks were going to be hired in the future. But on the campuses around town, black students were saying no to all the plans that did not express their viewpoint. And the way they were starting to see things wasn't as polite as the point of view of their elders. The students knew how long court cases took to be resolved. They knew that Negroes would be expected to *behave* during those times. They wanted a more dramatic sort of victory than others were willing to settle for; they wanted whites to come right out and say, We are wrong, we will stop being wrong *immediately*. Whites, on the other hand, said this kind of victory would humiliate them and was too much to ask.

The students were soon mobilizing themselves for some of the most forceful actions Negroes had ever put forth in the South. This was not to be an armed assault on the traditions of the South, it was to be a demonstrative expression directed at the hearts of all people of goodwill. The time had come to throw off the mask—not in secret and not in anger, but in peace and brotherhood and mutual respect. It could have happened that way. But it didn't.

One day during the late summer of 1957, a group of young black men in Atlanta boarded a city bus, rode for several blocks and were met by local police. Chief Herbert Jenkins himself was the arresting officer, and one of these young men, John Porters, was detained. Later he was booked, very quietly, and released. The case was now ready for court. Eventually two cases developed, one of them going directly to Federal District Court, the other being argued at the state level. A friend of M.L.'s, Sam Williams, who was president of the local chapter of the NAACP, was the plaintiff in the federal case. Atlanta's branch office of the NAACP was following the overall directive of the national headquarters, although Williams was reportedly favoring the pressure tactics of the sit-in movement. By now the divisions between the two movements had widened even further. The national civil-rights groups, by which I mean the NAACP and Urban League mainly, had no real interest in the nonviolent application of citizen protest if it constituted more than a single instance. They were, for example, more than satisfied with the extended period of time required to resolve the bus cases—two years. But to young people, that was an eternity for the right *to take a front seat on a bus*!!

When the bus cases were brought to court, Borders and the Wheat Street Baptist Church moved quickly, more quickly than anyone else, to pay some court costs, which the NAACP did not have the money to do. The emphasis thus shifted away from the value of NAACP rights tactics toward those of the younger strategists, who sought to force change to take shape more quickly. The state court upheld the bus company's right to segregate passengers, knowing that the federal court would overturn that decision. This helped whites save enough face to feel comfortable about the fact that they'd be sitting next to blacks when they all rode the city buses. The big question for all activists was how the fact of the southern timetable was to be taken into consideration in all future actions. If the buses took two years, many people were arguing, actual desegregation of the schools in response to the 1954 Supreme Court decision would take at least ten. The NAACP took the official position that the route through the courts was the only legitimate course to freedom. Fewer folks in the South seemed to be agreeing with them, however, as the Sixties approached. The power of new organizations was clearly evident now. Confrontation was a necessary part of the movement. To be put on hold when your life was at stake just wasn't going to be tolerated anymore. Many of us had hoped it would not come to such a point. And many knew that it had to.

Student demonstrations in other parts of the South brought Atlanta into a completely new political climate. There was no precedent for the size and scope of the changes Negroes were now demanding as part of their citizenship in this country. What could America tell the rest of the world about freedom if so many people in this country did not consider themselves free? And these young people could not be dismissed as troublemakers and hoodlums. Their grievances came out of acquired knowledge and experience. They were kids, but they were bright and sharp and filled with a sincere sense of purpose that seemed almost mystical at times. Before these believers, many others became cynics. It seemed naïve to suppose that hardened

southern whites could be reached with logical readings of the
U.S. Constitution, the Bill of Rights, or any other historical
evidence a person might honestly care to examine. But more
and more young people were moving together in the belief
that this *was* possible. And their faith was more than just con-
tagious. It embraced hundreds, then thousands, then hundreds
of thousands of people all over the country who now saw a
time when history could be shaped.

White resistance in Atlanta was predictably rigid. The businessmen were caught in the middle of their feelings and their
options. Many of them knew that northern corporations could
make fortunes from regional offices, franchised operations, and
subsidiary corporations throughout the South. Cities like Birmingham, New Orleans and Miami were all trying to compete for those dollars. Atlanta had the best shot at winning
if it could distinguish itself from all the others on the matter of race relations. Now those waters were being tested
by the Negro in a call to people of goodwill throughout the
world. We ask, said the students, that the world look to see if
we are being wronged in our country, and whether those
wrongs deserve international attention.

There could no longer be any question that they did. America
had to address itself to nations everywhere, not with slogans
about moving ahead slowly but surely, but rather with specific
actions to rid the most powerful country on earth of a crippling
disease for which a cure had always been available.

The businessmen of Atlanta responded hastily, without doing
what I think they might have done had they examined what
the students were asking for. Instead, they broke into factions
and tried to face individually what could only be solved by
everyone collectively. Richard Rich, head of the Atlanta department store that carried his family's name, came out of a
meeting and said he would not integrate his facilities until he
was assured that other store owners were committed to opening
their businesses to Negroes on an equal basis with whites. Rich,
I think, could have led the others; instead he tried to get them
to lead him. They couldn't. White reaction to a public statement in favor of integration by a small businessman could be
devastating; a man could lose a life's investment in a matter of

hours. Rich wouldn't be hit that hard, some of the smaller merchants felt.

It was here that a major imbalance in the struggle became evident. Whites were being represented, but blacks were producing leaders. The businessmen in white Atlanta were very entrenched sort of people, extremely conservative, basically distrustful of outsiders for all the friendly good ol' boy image projected across the country in movies and folk songs. Most of these men didn't even bother to consider what the changes would really accomplish. They lived with ideas that were then a hundred years old, and refused to take the kind of chance by investing in their own country that they were willing to take investing in a partnership in a frozen-custard stand. To represent them, they needed only men who would hold a line and not give anything up, not men who would seek, in an adventurous use of their own intellects, a philosophy of change and progress.

How sad it is, for example, that not a single white southern minister emerged to influence the spiritual development of whites living through the end of an old order and the start of a new one! Those of us in the Negro ministry counseled moderation for the very simple reason that we did not believe that bloodshed could be avoided; and once started, many of us felt, it would prove devastating. Why, we often asked each other, would whites want to risk that? What was it in them that could not face negotiating honorable terms with us? How easy it could have been. But someone, anyone with more than a loud voice going for him in the white community, had to *say* something!

Attorney A. T. Walden, one of the black leaders in the coalition, kept explaining to white coalition members how we had our hands full getting the student groups even to listen anymore. "They're kids," he'd shout, "and kids get impatient. You guys should know that from your own children!"

Direct action by students started in Atlanta after the year the bus cases were decided, 1960. Sit-ins and picket lines were organized by small groups working independently of any formal leadership. Eventually though, the students took their ideas and strategies to older leaders like Dr. Mays and myself. Both of us had concerns about the dangers involved. But Dr. Mays had been much more in touch then with events in places like Greensboro, North Carolina, where the sit-ins began, and told the young people to push forth with his blessings.

Hartsfield asked several of us to request the students to curtail the demonstrations for a month. Federal desegregation orders were being delivered to the Atlanta school system. That was going to build up some steam. Some of us disagreed in responding. Others said they'd work to set up a plan along those lines, which would have retained a few largely symbolic demonstrations instead of picketing and sit-ins. I didn't feel we could ask the students to do that. Any reduction of the size of their organizational efforts would appear to be a setback. And the students did react. Lonnie King, their leader and a former Morehouse student, vehemently opposed any changes in the direct-action programs that did not come from the activists themselves. He added some characterizations of the Voters' League members that were particularly uncalled for. When I tried to talk with him, we ended up heatedly denouncing each other. He was bullheaded and I was ready to compromise.

I wanted to compromise because that was the only way anybody in this thing was ever going to move. People had to start measuring what they were willing to give up, because it was time for just that. But if the whites gave up any part of segregation, they were going to be looking to save face on the issue. It was the thought of being humiliated that kept so many whites in the die-hard camp of segregation, I believe. Just the thought of having to say, Listen, I was wrong, let me make it up, was just too much. So the whole matter went out into the streets.

Many people in Atlanta had hoped that the bus-desegregation effort of 1957 would serve as the model for future civil-rights action in the city. But younger Negroes, especially the students of the Atlanta University System, were deeply impressed by the dynamic quality of the sit-in demonstrations that took place first in Greensboro, North Carolina, and then began to spread throughout the South. It was inevitable that this form of protest would reach Atlanta, although there was still considerable resistance to the direct-action process among both black and whites here.

During the early weeks of 1960, Lonnie King organized a group called the Committee on Appeal for Human Rights. In the beginning COAHR was content to follow the bus-desegregation model in its protests, and avoided any major confrontations with the white community. Until May of that year, Lonnie King was able to organize several marches and one sit-in at a local store without creating any situation that promoted violence. For a while the feeling was that Atlanta, true to many of its previous examples, would be able to offer change to the people without the overly dramatic encounters that were taking place in other southern cities. But these hopes were naïve. In mounting the first protests, Lonnie King had taken advice and counsel from the more experienced black leaders in the city. And because of that original relationship with us, integration plans were even supported, indirectly, by Hartsfield and Atlanta Police Chief Jenkins, who during these early protests instructed members of the force to arrest no one unless it became completely unavoidable. Had this mood been sustained, transitions from a segregated situation toward progress in racial matters might have been achieved without incident.

But at the state level there was not much of the sophistication that could be seen developing, however slowly, in Atlanta. The Georgia legislature, reacting, it seemed, to the vast amount of publicity Greensboro had received, passed an anti-trespass law in February. By enacting what they thought would be regarded as a show of strength, the lawmakers created another fortress to be attacked. By setting up another arrest mechanism, which said that the businessmen in town could have demonstrators picked up by police for not leaving a public place immediately when requested to do so by the owner, the Georgia state senators and representatives allowed a situation that was under control, partially at least, to grow completely out of hand. The students could see that whites intended to drown in the tide of history rather than give up the old ways that had kept them afloat in the past. Even the State Attorney General, Eugene Cook, insisted that Georgia was going to protect "individuals and their private rights." By individuals, he meant whites only. By private rights, he meant none that Negroes were assumed to have.

The attempt to integrate lunch counters that was spreading in the South was just a symbol, of course, but a clear one. There was great potential in this effort for addressing the larger issues, calmly, without hysteria, *if* the lunch counters could be seen in a proper perspective. But some reactions in the Negro community created tension between older and younger people.

C. A. Scott antagonized some of the students in the movement when he took to the editorial pages of his paper, the *Atlanta Daily World,* to call for more emphasis on "eliminating segregation in education . . . [along with] more voting and political influence; equal consideration in the administration of justice [as well as] improved economic opportunity . . ."

To the students, this was an empty viewpoint; it sounded reasonable but meant very little. Nothing in what Scott was telling them had a concrete issue at the center. The lunch counters, however insignificant they might have seemed to a man like Scott, who didn't use them anyway, were very real to the Negroes who were being humiliated every day because they could only afford such facilities for a snack or a meal when they were in the city's business areas. The students had also been growing up in a new atmosphere, one that many older Negroes were unfamiliar with. It wasn't lost on the younger people that the Supreme Court had been clear on the matter of school desegregation some six years earlier. To them, this was a long enough time to wait for a general action on the part of all people, an action to bring about all the changes America had been promising.

Lonnie King decided to model some demonstrations in Atlanta on the Greensboro sit-ins, and he formed a planning body with several Morehouse students, among them a young fellow named Julian Bond. Eventually, King and Bond were joined by another Morehouse man, Joe Pierce, in the planning of Atlanta's direct-action project.

Before moving ahead with their plans, the three young men visited Dr. Mays at Morehouse. He questioned only whether they felt able to handle such a project, and when assured by them that they could, he urged them to move on with it, with his full backing. Even then King, Bond, and Pierce didn't jump forward recklessly. They sought participation from others in the university. Presidents of the other member colleges couldn't back away from a time that clearly had come, but not all of them were quite as supportive as Dr. Mays. Later, he would graciously suggest that the other university heads had been with their students on the protest plans. But while the authority figures at Atlanta University never came right out with a rejection of what their young scholars wanted to do, some did stress to the students, over and over again, that college life was to focus on education. Anything else, some of the college presidents insisted, constituted little more than distraction. But even if they were somewhat reluctantly favorable, the leaders of A.U. were never so intimidated by possible white reaction that they expelled or otherwise pressured their students, which is the way it was in several black institutions across the South.

A dialogue was opened between the younger and older black factions in Atlanta, and out of the regular meetings they held throughout the winter months came a very new sense of political and social coalition. In addition to the students, men like Whitney Young, then Dean of the Atlanta School of Social Work, and Dr. Albert Manley, of Spelman College, used their experience as both educators and administrators to bring a solid foundation to the expression of Negro dissatisfaction with the southern condition.

Early in March of 1960 a statement by COAHR appeared. It was called "An Appeal for Human Rights," and was published by both of the city's white daily papers, the *Journal* and the *Constitution*, as well as by C. A. Scott's *Atlanta Daily World*. Lonnie King's group had been joined by representatives of the six member institutions of Atlanta University, the Urban League, and the NAACP in calling for an end to the segregated society southerners took for granted as a permanent condition. The appeal made it clear that freedom was the goal of those who had signed, nothing more and nothing less. Lonnie King's people were speaking out for their rights as American citizens and as human beings.

White response was largely stupid and irresponsible. Ernest

Vandiver, the governor of Georgia, labeled the appeal a Com-
munist-inspired piece of rabble-rousing. He went on to say
that no such thing as injustice existed in the city of Atlanta
where, after all, so many Negroes owned homes and ran their
own businesses. Some whites didn't speak out the way the
governor did, but his sentiments had a lot of support in Atlanta,
throughout the state, and in the rest of the South. Within the
Negro community, a new sense of unity between younger and
older people quickly developed. Those of us who had become
more economically secure than others knew that money and
social position didn't drive bigotry out of the lives of black
people. Many Negroes who had seen an attitude among young
folks that seemed *too* aggressive, *too* outspoken, were now rec-
ognizing the need for that sort of youthful energy and daring.

Not everybody in the Negro community was convinced of
this, however. C. A. Scott had printed the appeal in his paper
with some misgivings. He flatly rejected direct-action demonstrations as lawlessness that would never achieve what electoral
politics were bound to bring about in time. I believed in that
process, too, but I felt it was now too late for us to depend on
the ballot box exclusively in our efforts to change the South.

Many of the students had lost all faith in voting as a means
to an end. Those who still believed were weary from their many
disappointments with politicians and their empty promises. Two
clear paths had developed before us. I didn't feel, however,
that they had to be walked separately. In order to integrate our
society, we were going to have to integrate our strategies. Many
of Atlanta's veteran activists rejected this notion. The NAACP
and the Urban League adamantly refused to back direct action,
preferring to keep matters in the courts. Scott placed a wedge
between himself and the student groups when he called their
demonstrations foolish and editorialized in his newspaper:
". . . it seems necessary to refuse to make an issue at this
time over some of the less essential questions . . ."

The students and their leaders, Lonnie King in particular,
were angered by what they considered a put-down of their
efforts to integrate lunch counters and other public facilities
in town. Scott was trying, though, to make a very important
point when he wrote in the same editorial that the emphasis

in the struggle now had to be applied to ". . . the elimination
of segregation in education; more voting and political influence;
equal consideration in the administration of justice . . . and
improved economic opportunity."

Contrary to the beliefs of some people in Atlanta, Scott was
never—at least in my view—opposed to the students' goals, only
to their tactics. And in this, he was far from alone. The confusion came, I feel, because some of the students did not view
the demonstrations as a means for developing court cases, while
others did. There were those who felt that disruption was not
just a style but a philosophy within the movement. Disagreement over this issue remained central to the Civil Rights Movement and often divided it into several angry camps. Negotiations
were challenged by direct action. Churches became seriously
disrupted by differing attitudes within congregations. Where
I chose to be involved—even when I did not always agree with
those I joined with to continue the struggle—the Ebenezer family was right along with me. Many members had children in
college, youngsters who were taking an active part in the
demonstrations that would soon be seen around the world.

Direct action in Atlanta was rooted in nonviolence. Lonnie
King's leadership emphasized orderly, disciplined conduct by
the demonstrators, whose restraint in the face of relentless provo-
cation would remain unwavering. It was difficult. The name-
calling and the threats were clear and obvious. But it was the
hatred that whites directed at them that I think will remain
with so many of the students for all of their lives. Their question
was perhaps the same as mine for so many more years than
most of the students had been on earth: *Why?* What could
there possibly be that twisted the faces of housewives and office
workers into masks of fury and murderous rage? This anger
and rage frightened many of the students much more than
fear for their personal safety. All of us had to wonder just what
sort of people integration was going to bring Negroes into
contact with. And shortly after the publication of the Appeal
for Human Rights, a Federal District Court ruling helped
create even more tension throughout the city.

NAACP officials had requested a court order to require the
Atlanta school board to start integration efforts through a

pupil-placement plan. The court delayed the order for one year, from the fall of 1959 to the fall of 1960. Several days later, on March 15, 1960, Lonnie King and the student members of COAHR conducted a sit-in at several public places in downtown Atlanta, including several cateferias in federal office buildings. Seventy-seven demonstrators were arrested by both the city police and several county officials.

Reaction came quickly from both the black and white communities. Now that the appeal was being exercised as a plan of action, those who had praised it showered the students with stern criticism.

Editorial writers in the white press claimed the Negro cause had been set back. To where? some of us wondered. The newspapers also began to suggest somewhat regularly that school integration could only be delayed while these demonstrations continued . . . if they did.

Hartsfield now found himself in the position of having to speak out against all future demonstrations and other forms of direct action. Few Negroes in Atlanta were unmindful of the mayor's reputation as a moderate on racial issues. Black voters had supported him for more than a dozen years. But we now realized that even Hartsfield was unable to see what was developing, what had to happen. Asking us to pull back the demonstrations was like asking us to push rain back up into the sky. Somehow people in Atlanta had been convinced that the appeal would end all that the sit-in movement had come to represent. But young people had watched the bus-integration plan go into effect in Atlanta only after nearly two years of legal maneuvering. Nobody could wait that long again. And so when I was asked to stand bail for some of those arrested, the new day was upon me. White businessmen dug in and took a hard line. Some of them swore that Negroes would never eat in the white downtown restaurants, or even be able to enter the doors of some other establishments. Hartsfield urged several of us to curtail the direct-action projects that were in the planning stages. Police Chief Herbert Jenkins went to the Morehouse campus to assure students that Atlanta's police force would act with restraint during demonstrations.

I think it would be fair to say that by 1960, the major concern of most white southerners in cities like Atlanta was the matter of school integration. Little Rock and the massive resistance to integration that whites mounted there in 1957, when the President of the United States had to call out troops to maintain order in that city, was a serious reminder of just how much emotion was still involved in the process of ending segregation. Throughout the spring of 1960, the NAACP had pressed its suit to have the Atlanta school system begin the pupil-placement plan. The school board continued its appeal to the court, asking a one-year delay. In the spring, when a decision was to be handed down, demonstrations were continuing in downtown Atlanta. Just a few weeks earlier, in April, M.L. had spoken to a student gathering at Spelman College. These demonstrations, he told the crowd, must serve as a signal to all America that sitting in at lunch counters is just a beginning of our march for full freedom.

M.L. was now moving rapidly ahead toward the national leadership of a growing Civil Rights Movement that would soon be sweeping the nation. Many cheered him that night. But not everyone, I'm sure, knew just how much he'd really prophesied.

Thirteen

Nineteen sixty—a new decade, and another beginning for me. I was happy—M.L. was coming back to Atlanta! At the end of each phase of his education, I had tried to get him to join me in the pulpit at Ebenezer, but M.L. had always listened politely and patiently to my arguments and said, "No, Dad, not yet."

Now he and Coretta had spent five years at Dexter. They had enjoyed a beautiful and fulfilling experience in their first pastorate, and I thanked God for that. M.L. had successfully led the Montgomery Bus Boycott, which began as a local issue and drew national, then international attention. It also spawned other bus boycotts in the South, which led a group of clergy in 1957 to the founding of the Southern Christian Leadership Conference.

M.L. was elected president of SCLC, having no idea that the demands and responsibilities of the organization would increase as quickly as they did. He seemed to be on a marathon speaking schedule. His travel schedule was grueling, and more than once I said to him, "M.L., I don't see how you do it! You can't keep this pace going!" Because Atlanta continued to be the transportation hub of the South, he was constantly in the city making plane connections, and I began to think there might be some truth to the saying, "Even if you are going to heaven, you've got to come through Atlanta." The Southern Christian Leadership Conference was a national organization, and would continue to grow, with its headquarters in Atlanta, so M.L. accepted the call to come to Ebenezer as co-pastor with me.

So much had happened during these years. Early in 1955, Rosa Parks, returning home from a tiring day's work, refused to give up her seat on a city bus in Montgomery. She was arrested and the boycott that would bring world attention to Alabama began shortly afterward. Negroes had been abused, even shot, by Montgomery bus drivers. Incidents had been reported over many years. But whites there thought these things would pass by quietly, that Negroes in that part of America were too afraid to try to do anything about the conditions they had to live under. They were wrong, of course, and in being found out as people who *were* wrong, whites, in many instances, also became frightened. In 1956 my son's home in Montgomery was bombed while he was away at a rally. His wife and baby were inside, but fortunately were unhurt. Bunch received this news and was deeply pained by it. She wanted M.L. out of the movement right then. But I knew he would leave only when he felt he had accomplished what he set out to do. He'd grown up that way.

He'd been shaken by the bombing, but he was also determined to continue his work.

The model that Montgomery created for the movement could not always be duplicated in other cities. There was no coalition politics in Montgomery, no alliances or arrangements to channel grievances or negotiations. The boycott was an expression of discontent by black Americans that could only be answered publicly. In Montgomery there was no real line of communication between whites and blacks except in confrontation—the races there were so far apart. The 1956 victory in the bus boycott was a triumph over the coalition of ignorance and evil. The boycott gave black and white people a reason to see each other for what was really the first time. It required more than a year of people walking until many of them were nearly too tired to stand. But their determination was best expressed by the Negro woman who told a reporter asking her if the boycott wasn't taking a toll on her physically, "My feets is tired, but my soul is rested!"

The bus company stubbornly refused to accept the defeat of its segregationist policies and was eventually forced into bankruptcy after the Supreme Court ruled that its seating regulations were unconstitutional. M.L. had led the people of Montgomery in an achievement that ushered in the South's rebirth. It cost so much. But when it arrived, and people knew how uneasy our course was going to be from then on, there was no turning away, only the search for guidance and strength. The road ahead was clear enough. I remember how difficult the winter of 1956 was. When the city of Montgomery had branded him a criminal and an outlaw, M.L. became a symbol of black aspiration and a clear target for white hatred.

Earlier that year, I had received several telephone calls from whites I trusted, and each of them said my son's life was in danger. I just didn't believe them, I didn't want to. But while M.L. was speaking up in Nashville one night in February, indictments were delivered against him and several other members of the Montgomery Improvement Association, the group that had organized to coordinate the boycott. The Montgomery situation, I felt, was now out of hand, and when I picked M.L. up at the airport in Atlanta, where he'd come to be with Coretta and the baby, who were staying with us, I asked him not to go back. He said he had to. He'd accepted the MIA leadership and now he had to lead. I told him I thought it was too dangerous in Montgomery right now.

"Stay with us for a couple of weeks, M.L.," I said, knowing before I got the words out what his answer would be.

"Dad, I know Mother is sick with worry, and I don't want to add to that," he said. "But I've got to carry through on this. I don't really have a choice. We may not accomplish a great deal this time, I'm not sure. But it's a statement, Dad, it says we disapproved of something we felt had wronged us."

No one could persuade him to stay past the next morning. I invited several prominent men from our community over to talk with him, but their combined urgings to stay in Atlanta failed to sway M.L. Dr. Benjamin Mays, of Morehouse, whose influence had meant so much to M.L. when he was a student at the college, told him to go back if he had to and to expect his friends to help him all they could.

The others who spoke with M.L. that night included many old friends we both knew and respected. Their views, their wisdom and counsel meant a lot, although I knew by then that nothing in the world could change my son's mind. Men who were considered influential figures in Atlanta's leadership corps shared their experience and their knowledge with M.L. most of that evening. In addition to Dr. Mays, C. R. Yates, vice-president of Citizen's Trust, the third-largest black bank in America, was there, T. M. Alexander, an insurance broker, A. T. Walden, an attorney, Dan Duke, a white Atlanta attorney, Bishop S. L. Green of the A.M.E. Church of Georgia, and Rufus Clement, president of Atlanta University. They all spoke eloquently, and were at times tremendously persuasive, but no one was going to change M.L.'s direction that night.

Now it was a matter of living with him in this commitment. Clearly, the issue was no longer just a bus company in Montgomery. There was bound to be more. And nobody could really predict just how far whites would go to try to stop what was now becoming a mass movement drawing attention from around the world. All this considered, Bunch and I found it impossible to quiet our own fears for M.L.'s safety. The bombing of his home with his wife and child inside had just about torn his mother up emotionally. The jeopardy he placed himself in constantly made us apprehensive now of every ring of our telephone.

It was the beginning of many unhappy, anxious hours we would spend, Bunch and I, waiting for word, hoping that no madman had found a way to M.L.'s door. But we could only support what he chose to do. Bunch often said that she would never fail to stand with him, though she was not always in agreement with the ways the movement chose to accomplish its work. But she'd grown up in her father's house, hearing him preach and plan as he sought to bring about the fall of southern segregation. So, of course, she knew it was useless to try to persuade others to do what M.L. had now learned he was most

capable of doing: providing leadership when it was clearly
needed. His preaching was rich with spirit and power. He could
move people with great, rolling thunder in his voice, the words
moving smoothly from him and reaching people with the enormous conviction that all speakers who can move masses of
human beings bring to the simplest sentence. He was becoming
a national leader because it was time for this to happen, and
time, of course, for it to happen to Martin Luther King, Jr.

I could only be deeply impressed with his determination.
There was no hesitancy for him in this journey. M.L. told us all
that he was returning to Montgomery because he would rather
go back there and spend ten years in jail than not go back.

I drove M.L., Coretta, and the baby, Yolanda, over to Montgomery the next morning. I think we'd all spent a very restless,
troubled night. It was very quiet in the car as we traveled. We
were met by the Reverend Ralph Abernathy, an early and close
associate of M.L.'s in Montgomery, and elsewhere as the movement spread across the country. Along with several dozen others,
M.L. and Ralph Abernathy had been charged with "interfering
with the normal business of the Montgomery bus lines." They
were booked, fingerprinted and photographed as though the city
wanted folks there to believe that my son and the boycott were
some kind of menace to society. But it wasn't until weeks had
passed and the trial of the boycott leaders was under way and
the nation and the world watched a cruel, immoral system un-
fold as the testimony of witness after witness spilled out of the
Montgomery courthouse. M.L. had told me there was no way
they could win the case given the law as it was established—
the boycott leaders were "guilty." But that trial, as many others
would, laid bare the bones of the system and shocked some people who had been its strongest supporters.

Now, in the 1960s, M.L. had come back home. I again
urged him to cut back on his activities, take a long look at
the way things were developing before he exposed himself to
the constant danger that gathered around him. Several times
we argued. I'd grow angry, telling him how bullheaded he was
being. He'd been scarred by the struggle in very serious ways.
His schedule—the speaking, the organizing, the meetings—had

exhausted him. In 1958, while signing autographs of his first book, *Stride Toward Freedom*, he was stabbed by a deranged Negro woman in a Harlem department store. After recovering, in 1959 he and Coretta accepted an invitation from the Gandhi Peace Foundation and spent several weeks in India, where they met and conferred with men and women who had known Mahatma Gandhi and who advised M.L. on the history and practice of nonviolent protest. He returned to the United States filled with energy, wanting more than ever to extend civil rights into America's future.

By 1960, student involvement in the struggle was moving individuals and groups apart philosophically. At a student meeting held in Raleigh, North Carolina, that April, the Student Nonviolent Coordinating Committee (SNCC) was formed to continue the direct-action phase of the movement. In Raleigh, M.L. called for nonviolent sit-ins that would lead to mass arrests, filling the jails of the South with activists who would refuse to post bail. Other leaders there questioned the nonviolent approach. The division resulted in SNCC's wanting to move with more haste than SCLC, though still nonviolent in its approach; less interested in the process of negotiation than in the power to unsettle the white power structure throughout the South. But with young people, the pendulum will swing back and forth. Often the students changed their tactics and veered between the two basic ideologies: encounter and debate.

M.L. was being arrested almost regularly now. A.D., who'd left business for preaching and had accepted a pastorate in Newnan, Georgia, joined his brother at a lunch counter sit-in in Atlanta during the fall of 1960. They were both arrested, along with seventy others. M.L. refused to post bail; so did the rest of those arrested. Hartsfield asked for a two-month truce on the demonstrations in exchange for releasing everyone from jail. The others were let go, but M.L. was detained by officials of nearby De Kalb County, who took him from Atlanta in handcuffs before Judge Oscar Mitchell in county court, charging that M.L. had violated his probation for an old traffic charge—when he first moved back to Atlanta, he had neglected to transfer his driver's license from Alabama to Georgia. He had been fined and given a suspended sentence. When I appealed to Mitchell for a real hearing on this matter, he said, with a laugh: "I don't have time, I'm going fishing . . ."

M.L.'s attorney, Donald Hollowell, was unable to convince the judge that convicting M.L. in this way was not an instance of justice being served, either for my son or for the people of Georgia. Mitchell sentenced M.L. to serve four months at hard labor in the state prison at Reidsville. Hollowell went off to prepare an appeal, and during the night, without any notice to the attorney or our family, my son was taken in chains to Reidsville. Now our struggle was against the history of the South, and there was deep concern among us regarding M.L.'s safety. Reidsville was several hours away by car. My son was being taken down there in the middle of the night along those lonely Georgia roads, where nearly anything dangerous was possible.

He arrived at the prison, and through contacts around the state I was able to learn that the authorities were hoping to create a situation that would result in M.L.'s being killed in a fight with another inmate at Reidsville. Later, according to this plan, much regret would be expressed over the incident, and it would be looked upon as one of those unfortunate things that sometimes happen. When Coretta called me the next morning—A.D. had gone to the county jail to see his brother and had been told he was on the way to Reidsville—she was fighting to remain composed. A.D. had called her as soon as he knew; his mood was one of anger and frustration.

Coretta was unaware of the reputation this rural prison had earned over a period of several years. It was a place for hardcore criminals, many of them in need of professional help with emotional problems, and it was also an institution with a staff that seemed at times to live for the possibility of forcibly controlling the prisoners.

"Dad," Coretta cried, "what's going to happen to him down there?"

She knew, as we all did, that M.L. was never comfortable in isolation. He enjoyed people too much to be cut off from others without suffering enormous anxiety. If they put him in solitary confinement, I felt, the effects on his well-being might be devastating. Worse than anything else, perhaps, they had taken M.L.

away from Coretta and his family during her pregnancy with their third child.

I now made contact with Morris Abram, a prominent attorney in Atlanta and a man whose political contacts I felt would prove invaluable under the prevailing circumstances. And they were. I've been criticized severely over what happened next, but for all the years following those days, I've never regretted what I did. I knew the jeopardy my son was in. The Deep South was burning with a furious spiritual flame. For Negroes it was a fire lit for freedom. Whites experienced the heat of resistance. They were defending the impossible, trying to put a sack over tomorrow morning's sunrise to keep it from shedding the light a new day was bringing.

I was headed out the door of my home on the way to a meeting with Mr. Abram when Bunch called me back to the phone. Coretta had received a call from Massachusetts Senator John F. Kennedy, the Democratic party's candidate for President in the upcoming elections. For a number of personal reasons, I had been more impressed, at that point anyway, by the Republican nominee, Richard Nixon, who was then Vice-President under Dwight Eisenhower. My political beliefs, then as now, included a willingness to vote man and not party.

Coretta described Senator Kennedy's expression of concern over what was going on with M.L.'s imprisonment. The Senator was not alone in his apparent alarm over the clear violation of basic legal principles that Judge Mitchell had practiced. Word had also reached the White House, where both President Eisenhower and Vice-President Nixon moved back and forth between using their influence and saying nothing. Finally, they both declined comment. In their view, apparently, any intervention in what they regarded as a state matter would be unwise. They sat on their hands and never offered so much as a gesture toward Georgia.

Then Senator Kennedy's brother Robert telephoned Judge Mitchell to ask why bail hadn't been granted in a case that, after all, involved no serious crime. Suddenly papers were signed on M.L.'s behalf and a day later, my son had been released from prison.

A mass meeting was held at Ebenezer the night that M.L. was released. I told the crowd that I'd been deeply impressed by the Kennedys during this especially trying period. John and Robert had acted with moral courage, I felt, and stood up to be counted for what they, and all people of goodwill, knew was right.

And I said from the pulpit that, "Yes, if *I* had a suitcase full of votes, I'd hand them over to John Kennedy, hoping he could use them in the upcoming election." I don't know if that statement influenced many Negro voters across the country or not. Kennedy won, of course, and it is history that he won by a very small margin. I was pleased, frankly. Kennedy's presidency opened some doors, although it left some others closed. But he acted when he saw an opportunity. And I said: More power to him. M.L. never offered a formal statement on behalf of Kennedy's candidacy. He expressed his thanks and said very little more. He was out of Reidsville, but there was still so much work to do.

These were times when the nation and many parts of the world listened to much of what was being said in our southern pulpits. And I do recall saying that although I wasn't urging anything on anyone else, I felt strongly now about the upcoming election and my support of a presidential candidate. And, I told the audience, stressing the word *if*: If I had a suitcase full of votes, I'd dump as many of them as he could hold right in John Kennedy's lap!

I don't know just who heard me. And I'll never really be sure that those who did were seriously influenced. But John Kennedy did come from behind in the polls that year to beat Nixon by an extremely narrow margin.

It was said the Kennedys put one over on us because we weren't really astute enough to see how we were being used. Oh, we were called blind and ignorant. But I remind those who said this then and may believe it now just what the alternative was. I did what I felt was necessary. And I still feel in my heart that anyone who would have hesitated to welcome the help the Kennedys offered has never had a son or daughter in the kind of danger M.L. faced at Reidsville. I'm quick to add, however, that I don't believe the real danger came from the prisoners. When M.L. left the prison, after a brief press conference down there, several prisoners reportedly shouted after him: "Long live the King!" If it had come to that, I believe those men down there would have protected him as far as might have been required—all the way. So many folks, from so many parts of American society, looked upon this young King as somebody whose presence and whose safety was vital.

As M.L. continued to develop his leadership, Bunch and I felt a degree of jealousy emerging from people within our own community. Many felt M.L. was receiving too much personal publicity at the expense of others who were contributing significantly to the struggle. If any of this were true, and I've never believed it was, M.L. certainly wasn't to blame for it. He had no control over newspaper and television coverage of anything he said or did. Often he was misquoted, or partial statements were printed that didn't carry the spirit of what he had to say.

An extraordinary group of young men and women was emerging in the Civil Rights Movement. M.L. was fortunate in having drawn around him numbers of people who possessed tremendous vision and skill. As the movement brought public attention to small towns like Albany, Georgia, and cities like Birmingham, young people left an impression upon the country linked to voting and integrated public facilities and schools. M.L. introduced me to such young people as Wyatt Tee Walker, John Lewis, another young minister named Andrew Young, to the Fred Shuttlesworths, the Ella Bakers and Julian Bonds who worked to keep this American society alive and healthy. The courage of young people like Charlayne Hunter and Hamilton Holmes, who faced terror tactics day and night when they integrated the University of Georgia in 1961, made a big impression on all of us. Likewise all of the workers in all of the organizations that registered thousands of Negro southerners to vote when it could cost lives even to discuss the ballot box. To some this was a period of turmoil; I saw it as one of the great periods of America's history. Atlanta began to grow as it never had before, attracting young men and women, blacks and whites, to bring their dreams and their hopes to the South and its future.

This drive to freedom often hurt. The cost was high for every step forward we took. And while violence was kept away from

Atlanta to a greater extent than in many large cities in both the
North and South, the pain was felt everywhere that our struggle continued. There were still times when I shouted in meetings or walked out of them. But I think a solid, progressive
leadership saved a lot of heartache in Atlanta—not all of it, but
a lot.

M.L. and the SCLC were in disagreement with such men as
Thurgood Marshall, then the NAACP's legal counselor, and
later a Supreme Court Justice, who felt that SCLC proposals
to use high-school students in the demonstrations against segregated schools were unwise. This was the start of a continuing
disagreement on tactics between M.L. and the major leaders of
the large civil-rights groups: men like the NAACP's longtime
executive director, Roy Wilkins, and Lester Granger and his
successor as head of the Urban League, Whitney Young.

Basically, I believe, these men felt that M.L.'s efforts to bring
the poor directly into the process that would eventually liberate
them conflicted with their own plans to leave planning and im-
plementation of rights programs to professionals. This was a division that never subsided. But some of us did feel that after a
brilliant victory in the *Brown* v. *the Board of Education* case
before the Supreme Court, the NAACP tended toward a conservative path. They had placed more faith in the U.S. courts
than those institutions might have deserved in America's twentieth century.

Even so, when M.L. first returned to Atlanta, and he and
Coretta and their babies stayed with us awhile, we argued about
his choice of methods. I felt I knew more about southern danger
than he did, but he'd respond by saying that if this were true it
still could not move him away from the responsibility he'd assumed. Both M.L. and his brother inherited a lot of stubborn-
ness from somewhere in the family. And where I had succeeded
in convincing A.D. that he should return to his studies and to
eventual pastorates in Newnan, Georgia, Birmingham, Alabama,
and Louisville, Kentucky, M.L. moved through his adult life
without my instruction.

"It is clear," M.L. had written back in 1956, "that the Negro
is in for a season of suffering."

Although the Civil Rights Movement never sought to tear

down the United States, those of us who participated actively in it were often regarded as traitors and subversives. Black people in this nation know that the season M.L. spoke of has not yet ended. In the Sixties it seemed to appear anew every day. The murders, the bombs in homes and churches, the killing of little children should offer more than enough evidence as to just who was subversive. The movement in all of its phases and various philosophies recognized a deteriorating United States of America that was ripping itself in half across the color line. The survival of Negroes was basic to the survival of this country. And for this reason our battle could not end quickly; there were so many issues connected to the unity of people in this country. Divisions had brought us close enough to disaster. Negroes could not move forward without the rest of America moving in the same direction. Whites did not always think of us as patriots, but that's what the Civil Rights Movement really was made up of . . . men and women who believed in this society when it did not believe in them.

One vital dimension that was often overlooked in the assessments of this period was the concern throughout black America for excellence, scholarship, and the general advancement of Negroes within a nation that was itself advancing. And we saw so many people ignoring U.S. racial policy, or looking at it as an insignificant matter. These things weakened the country. American kids began to question whether anything they were being told by their parents was true if the lie of race was so nakedly displayed. The generations lost contact with one another. Confidence was lost and in some instances not restored. Americans became suspicious, isolated, and violent. The lie kept on devouring us as a country because we would not slay the dragon that it was, we would not move to the basic truth that until all of us were full citizens, none could be, and that any who thought otherwise played on themselves a terrible deception.

We could end the deception. But as a people we'd have to be stronger than we'd ever been before.

Fourteen

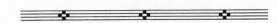

August 1960 was an extremely joyful month for our family. Christine was now teaching at Spelman College, and doing very well. Sometime during 1957, she'd met a young journalist from Missouri, Isaac Newton Farris, at a wedding reception of some mutual friends in Atlanta. He was a good-looking young fellow, and I liked his confidence, his solid hold on personal convictions. They began dating. Christine had brought a few suitors home for me to meet. I hadn't been terribly impressed with any of these fellows. But an incident one evening convinced me that this young man Isaac Farris was made of a little better stuff. They'd gone to see a movie and stopped for coffee afterward. They were in love. Time passed, and Christine, who was living at home with us, got in pretty late.

Now there were a few young men who'd heard my voice get big when they brought Christine and the boys back late from dances and parties when they were teenagers. I was waiting up for her, thinking that my sharp words were going to be for my daughter's ears alone. But young Farris had come in to be sure I understood that he'd bear any responsibility for the lateness

of the hour. And he wasn't humble about it, either. He stood straight up, looked me in the eye and said, "Good evening, Reverend King. I'm Isaac Newton Farris from Eolia, Missouri, and I'm in love with your daughter and plan to marry her if she's agreeable and you are."

Well, I chuckled, he was such a solid young fellow, a true man, I felt right away. More than anything else, he seemed like family from the first moment we talked.

On August nineteenth, her brothers performed Christine and Isaac's wedding at Ebenezer. And to this day I'd like to meet the man who's ever gained a finer son-in-law. His strength would become a rock in times of need we'd be experiencing up ahead. What I like about him most of all, I think, is that he knows how to hold on to who he is without making any fuss, quietly, firmly, with a lot of old-fashioned American spine.

The South had changed a great deal during William Hartsfield's administration as mayor of Atlanta. He was returned to office term after term, serving twenty-three years altogether. The Atlanta airport was named after him, which was fitting because I think he always considered bringing major airline terminals to the city his most important achievement. In my view, he had accomplished other things. He'd been an unusually effective leader during an especially difficult time. He tried to walk a line between two opposing forces and he did that as well as any elected official could have done it at that time. When he stepped down as mayor, I realized the years had rushed past. I had entered my sixties, and I knew the time was now coming when my participation in church and civic activities would have to be cut back.

What I wanted more than anything else now was to play out the grandfather role my own children had been creating for me. A.D. and Naomi were now proud parents of nine-year-old Alveda, eight-year-old Alfred Daniel Williams King II, and Derek Barber and Esther Darlene who were six and four. And in M.L. and Coretta's home there were Yolanda Denise and Martin III, and Dexter Scott was on the way. Yolanda and Marty had been born during those especially trying times in Montgomery. And there were more grandchildren to come. Bernice

would be born to M.L. and Coretta in early 1963, Vernon to
A.D. and Naomi in the fall of 1960. Christine and Isaac would
have their Isaac, Jr., in the spring of 1962, and Angela Christine during the spring of 1964. So I felt I had a career. I started
my new life as Daddy King.

I was helpless before the little ones; children just fascinated
me. Bunch tried to keep me from spoiling the whole crowd as it
grew, but I knew they'd always look to Grandaddy for the soft
touch in their lives; I just couldn't resist them. So much seemed
to be contained in the presence of that generation. All the work,
the years gone by in great struggle, I would always see in their
little faces, in those climbing, jumping bodies as they grew up
all around me. I knew I'd never tire of them as long as I was
here, and I planned with each arrival to be around just that
much longer. God was on His job when He made me. The Lord,
I was certain, had been plowing deep ground when He put me
together there in the country. I was put here, as the old folks
would say, on a purpose. I'd been sent here to preach, and if I
had sold *me* back in those times when I thought about being in
some sort of business operation, the riches might have come to
me in another way—in cash dollars only.

My present riches were far more valuable. Because it took
more than breath and britches to be a preacher who brought a
church along and grew, as the church grew with him. And so
I measured my life in gladness. I had been bothered, worried
and disturbed, but I had never used any of this as an excuse to
hate anyone. I was most proud of that. When it came to what
we'd had to struggle to achieve, I'd fussed about all things and
never pulled back from arguing about them. And if I wasn't a
great preacher, I sure was a good one, and I put myself forth as
best I could, always. My memories were valuable. I'd always
have them as my personal wealth. And it could only increase.

As the Sixties unfolded, the great well of passion stored up in
this country for so long simply spilled over. M.L. and A.D. were
moving the South with their efforts and those of the young men
and women who marched America far beyond its own expecta-
tions for a time. And whether the location was Albany, Georgia,
or Birmingham, Alabama, or Chicago, Illinois, the message was
clear. The cause of integration in America was served by the na-

tion's aristocrats, farmers and students, by workers and preachers, men and women, young and old. The costs were accepted
when they came and they were often very high. But we moved
through.

Ivan Allen, who succeeded Hartsfield as mayor, had the
courage to stay in office for a couple of terms, and it took
courage through the Sixties. The Voters' League was with him
and with Sam Massell, the city's first Jewish mayor, who succeeded him. And coming into the present, Atlanta has a black
mayor, Maynard Jackson, whose grandfather, John Wesley
Dobbs, and I labored together in the Thirties and Forties to
make it possible for our people to vote. I've supported that line
of succession with the long-term feeling that it may be the most
interesting series of city officials in the nation's history. So I
have lived in Atlanta, and go on doing so.

I also lived to be at Oslo, Norway, to bear witness when M.L.
received the Nobel Prize for Peace in 1964. And I prayed on
the plane trip over there that the Lord would keep me humble,
the son of a sharecropper and father of a man who, at the age
of thirty-five, had been presented the most prestigious of world
awards. God surely had looked down into Georgia. And He
must have said, Well, here are people I will give a mission
and see how well they can carry it out. And I felt He must have
looked down into Oslo, Norway, and simply said, Yes, they have
shouldered the weight part of the way. A people had been led
by a young man who could have found comfort elsewhere, yet
stayed where he was needed, bearing witness. And as M.L. stood
receiving the Nobel Prize, and the tears just streamed down my
face, I gave thanks that out of that tiny Georgia town I'd been
spared to see this and so much else. M.L. was my co-pastor
now, and A.D. would soon be joining us in serving Ebenezer.
I knew the movement was far from finished with its work, but I
did feel M.L. had given so much, reached so deeply inside himself to be up in the front lines, where the glory was thought to
be, but where danger held the real dominion.

Killing is a contagion. It begins, then rushes like fire across
oil, raging through emotions out of control. America will have
to remember the early Sixties when the guns came out, when

small children were blown to pieces while in church, and the blood seemed destined to flow until it became a river. The nation seemed to lose its way, as though it stumbled for a while through some dense forest where nothing could be seen clearly. How could we not have realized what was coming when those four young girls were killed by the explosion at their church in Birmingham? Was it not any clearer when civil-rights workers began disappearing, and when Medgar Evers, over in Mississippi, was shot down without any real concern about punishing the man who supposedly murdered him? How could a nation have not understood the terrible path it was walking when the President of the United States could be gunned down while riding in an open car through an American city?

The turmoil continued. The Sixties were a time of battle for jobs and housing and the winning over of whites, who came now to understand how their lives, too, were being bent out of shape.

What we learn, with God's help, is that there is no safety. Therefore, there can be no danger we are not willing to face. A great passion stirred this nation in the Sixties, bringing violence and rage with it, but focusing on the hypocrisy that was at the root of America's racial condition. Our struggle against that racist part of the nation's personality was recognized, in some instances, more quickly and with a great deal more understanding in other parts of the world than it was at home.

When M.L. asked me to join him in 1964 at Oslo for the Nobel ceremonies, all over Europe folks had been clearly aware of what my son was trying to accomplish against enormous odds. But in the United States, a campaign to destroy his leadership was conducted within the government. J. Edgar Hoover, head of the FBI, made no secret of the fact that he held M.L. and his work in contempt. And the Civil Rights Movement received little active support from church leaders, many of them close enough to the struggle to see how important M.L.'s nonviolent protests had become among young people. When he was in jail, there were those who turned their backs, who criticized and rebuked him. He carried on.

It was a time when strong churchmen needed to reach out to embrace the American public as it huddled against its pain and tried to pretend that everything was still under control. We had moved to establish the sense of freedom any people must have to remain civilized. I had entered civic affairs as a young man because I thought everyone wanted a better world and that nobody would have one if I didn't put a shoulder to all the wheels that turned justice and dignity. A preacher, as I understood the term, was called for life. And there was a wondrous harvest in those fruitful years. But I could hear the ticking that was fast replacing the American heartbeat in our daily lives. And as M.L. expanded the movement, I became more and more concerned and less and less able to get him to pull back even for a time. Bunch was deeply affected, of course. She grew ever more apprehensive as her sons became rooted in the struggle and the cause.

By 1968, there was great anxiety throughout our family. No matter how much protection of any sort a person has, it will not be enough if the enemy is hatred that cannot be turned around. Not even the forces of law can control such hatred in a society. When evil is organized, it becomes a cup more bitter than the one given Jesus . . .

In April 1968, my sons went to Memphis to help organize a struggle by the city's sanitation workers to achieve better wages and working conditions. I wondered about M.L.'s involvement in this, whether or not he was spreading his concerns and his energies too thin. But again he was right. There could be no real separation between exploiting a man because of his color and taking advantage of his economic condition to control him politically. Exploitation didn't need to be seen only in terms of segregation. It involved all people, white and black, in the continuing human drive toward freedom, toward personal dignity within a just society. In Memphis, M.L.'s joint efforts with the workers brought out the old charge that he was, inside, more Communist than Baptist, which may have been the silliest thing anybody ever said about any person in America.

M.L. had been able to convince his brother, who was extremely skeptical in the beginning, that he too could make a difference in the kind of America that would enter the twenty-first century. The nation could be changed. The cracks in the armor of racist attitudes were visible all over the South. Maybe the time had been ripe before, but M.L. could see that now was an excellent moment in history to move a nation beyond itself. He sensed that Americans would respond emotionally to what he was now doing, that their passions could be cooled, then turned around into a force that would make the country into the place it should always have been. We have the resources, he would explain to me. We have the means, and the human energy needed is at its peak. . . .

The tension of those months took a heavy toll on Bunch, who was always aware of the pressure both the boys were under in their daily lives. The sound of a telephone, our doorbell ringing, any call that brought with it some news, edged up on us like a series of loud, sudden alarms. M.L. knew he had to share with his mother the changing nature of events as they involved him. Each moment he was away, out of touch with her, became an eternity of waiting for the next indication of any kind that he was all right.

He came to Atlanta and had dinner one evening with his mother and me. Some of the things he'd told me earlier came as no surprise, but both of us understood how difficult the information was going to be for Bunch to handle. Several reliable sources, both private and from within the federal government, concluded that attempts would soon be made on M.L.'s life. Money was involved. Professional killers were being recruited.

After dinner, the three of us sat out on our patio and enjoyed the late-setting sun of a warm, clear evening. Had I chosen M.L.'s words, perhaps I wouldn't have been so blunt. He felt, though, that out of respect for his mother, he couldn't be less than candid with her. "Mother," he said, "there are some things I want you to know."

She didn't want to listen, not then, on that quiet Sunday when it was so good to laugh about childhood, and remember tears easily replaced with laughter back when everything seemed so much less dangerous.

"There's a chance, Mother, that someone is going to try to kill me, and it could happen without any warning at all." M.L. said this quickly, then stood up and walked to the far end of the patio. We sat silently, knowing that for this moment at least there couldn't be any words. The same emotions that caused

Bunch and me to urge M.L. to leave the movement more than ten years before were all still there. But saying these things now could bring no relief, only an intensity to the suffering we all carried. The great weight of that, I still believe, came from the certainty all of us had that what M.L. had chosen to do was unquestionably right.

We had been aware of the dangers, each out of our own experiences with the South we knew—M.L., his mother and I. A time had come. To avoid it was impossible, even as avoiding the coming of darkness in the evening would have been impossible. But word was moving through our part of the world. People were reporting conversations overheard in restaurants, in taverns, on street corners, that indicated serious efforts to plot against M.L. as a leader of this movement that was changing so much in America so quickly. Police departments had been alerted. The talk of hired killers being on the loose and following M.L. was now past the stage of rumor and hearsay. Police officers who had never been in sympathy with our cause were nevertheless concerned about anything happening to my son in one of their towns or cities. It simply wouldn't have looked good, I suppose, for all these law-and-order advocates to be unprepared for lawbreakers whose intention was to commit murder.

"But I don't want you to worry over any of this," M.L. said, returning to his mother's side. "I have to go on with my work, no matter what happens now, because my involvement is too complete to stop. Sometimes I do want to get away for a while, go someplace with Coretta and the kids and be Reverend King and family, having a few quiet days like any other Americans. But I know it's too late for any of that now. And if mine isn't to be a long life, Mother, Dad, well then I respect that, as you've always taught us to respect it as God's will."

We ached when he left that evening, deep inside, and though we tried to comfort each other with small talk about neighbors and church folks and even our earliest hours together, nothing could remove the unspoken pain we were sharing.

M.L. went back to Memphis, and Bunch was cheered by the consideration he and A.D. showed for her in this difficult time by calling during the day, just to assure her things were going fine. They seemed closer to each other now than at any time while they were growing up. A.D. grew strong in his role as brother. M.L. could now depend on him as never before, and even with all his trusted and valuable staff, the presence of his family in A.D. kept his spirit up so much of the time when this, more than anything else, was needed. They would both be on the phone with their mother, laughing and riding each other about their huge appetites and what they were doing to their respective waistlines. But that did not stop M.L. from saying, "Mother dear, I will be in Atlanta on Saturday, and I want you to cook some barbeque for me. I'll come to your house for dinner." It must have seemed that with all the power that affection generated, there would be some haven of safety.

A.D. now had found his calling. He was firm in his *own* sense of ministry, confident both in what he could and could not do. He was not his brother, and not his father either, but now it was finally clear that he was going to be the finest Alfred Daniel Williams King the world would ever know.

Bunch was in good humor as we drove to Ebenezer that Thursday evening of April fourth, 1968, although our Ebenezer family had been saddened during the week by the unexpected death of Mrs. Ruth Davis, who had been one of M.L.'s Sunday school teachers, and the passing, in Detroit, of Mrs. Nannien Crawford, a trustee of the church. The next week, Mrs. Crawford's daughter died, and I knew it was my responsibility to preach the funeral of each of the members, and God gave me the strength to do what I had to do. The boys had called Bunch twice before noon, just to pester her, they said. M.L. was going to speak that night, and he wanted more than anything else for his mother to know that she shouldn't take the television reports of the danger he was in too seriously. Things were shaping up much better than he had expected. Several Negro police officers were looking after him, even during their off-duty hours. For the moment, anyway, there seemed very little to worry about.

Ebenezer is a busy church, and we were there almost every evening for a scheduled activity. When we arrived at the church, Bunch and I found our car's path into the parking lot next to the church blocked by a driver who kept honking the horn and pointing to me as she yelled something neither of us could understand because her car window was up. I motioned for her to roll it down, but several other cars were now backed up along Auburn Avenue and the woman suddenly pulled away, thinking, I suppose, that we'd understood what she was trying to tell us. I parked, and Bunch and I rushed into the church building. We went upstairs to my study without exchanging a word, and I turned on the radio near my desk. M.L. had been shot, an announcer was saying, and he'd suffered a very serious wound.

I turned to Bunch. She was calm, but the tears had started pouring down her face. No sound came, though. The crying was silent as we waited for more specific news. I began praying, filling the study with my words. Soon more news had been received by a local radio station that indicated M.L. was hurt but still alive. Another report came through, saying the bullet had struck him in the shoulder, and I heard myself asking, "Lord, let him live, let him be alive!" But moments later the newscaster had a final, somber bulletin: Martin Luther King, Jr., had been shot to death while standing on a balcony at the Lorraine Motel in Memphis. Again, I turned to Bunch. Neither of us could say anything. We had waited, agonizing through the nights and days without sleep, startled by nearly any sound, unable to eat, simply staring at our meals. Suddenly, in a few seconds of radio time, it was over. My first son, whose birth had brought me such joy that I jumped up in the hall outside the room where he was born and touched the ceiling—the child, the scholar, the preacher, the boy singing and smiling, the son —all of it was gone. And Ebenezer was so quiet; all through the church, as the staff learned what had happened, the tears flowed, but almost completely in silence.

Christine and Isaac flew to Memphis with Coretta, in a private airplane graciously provided for our use by Senator Robert Kennedy. It was a difficult experience for two women not used to the rush of questions from reporters, the blazing TV lights, the crowds pressing everywhere to get a look at a family in distress.

I still often wonder how Christine and Coretta held up so well, but they stood proud and composed throughout so much of the frenzy that followed the report of M.L.'s death. Isaac provided a quiet, firm presence, and his great strength in the middle of so much pressure was invaluable. They were accompanied on the trip to Memphis by Jean Young, Andy's wife, and some other friends, including Dora McDonald, Fred Bennette, and Ralph Abernathy's wife, Juanita.

The outpouring of sympathy was the greatest that the city of Atlanta had ever witnessed. Atlanta was magnificent! The eyes of the world were on the city, and it was at its best. I am told that if an organization had been planning a convention at which there would be as many people as had come to M.L.'s funeral, the planning would have started at least five years in advance. Atlanta had only a few hours to prepare for the multitude that thronged the city—a multitude of humanity, the influential, such as Governor Nelson Rockefeller, the Vice President of the United States, Hubert Humphrey, governors, mayors, senators, congressmen, high officials of every major organization of goodwill in the world; and the nameless poor, those valiant men and women who had marched with M.L. from Montgomery to Memphis—they all came, and Atlanta opened its heart to them. It was the city's finest hour.

They brought my son home to Atlanta, to a funeral that gathered up America's attention for a day. One day in exchange for so many others. Yet we said again that God is good. I reached down for my son during the services and cried out to him: "M.L.! Answer me, M.L."

But that hour when we could speak is gone. And that ache I thought would not ever leave gradually subsides. I remember the children, and all the work we must continue doing so that they never lose faith in the rightness of what's been done in their names.

M.L.'s death was a terrible blow for all of us. I came to admire my wife's great personal strength during this period. She suffered enormously, but never neglected to be available to others in the family who needed her. Our marriage had always been rather exceptional, I think. We seldom argued, we shared laughs with each other, we had cried together and never exchanged bitterness or hatred. Couples who are together a long time come through these ways. I counseled many of them as a minister. More than a few surprised me with the antagonisms they felt for each other. How, I often wondered, have these people managed to live together in the same house for five minutes, let alone a lifetime?

So, I had always felt marriage was an institution that had provided me with many blessings. The warmth and quiet passion that moved between Bunch and me gave me a grand and often wondrous life on this earth. I have never stopped feeling that grandness, that fortunate state I was able to occupy.

We traveled, Bunch and I, to places that were not so special in themselves at times but that gave us an opportunity to be alone with our contemplations and, at times, our pain. In the months after M.L. died, of course, we stayed with family matters, answering thousands of expressions of sorrow from around the world. But at some point, I realized that even at sixty-eight years of age, I still had a lot of preacher in me. So I went on with that, and lived my life with Bunch and the family. The grandchildren were growing faster than their parents had, it seemed.

In September of 1968, A.D., my second son, was installed as co-pastor of Ebenezer. A.D. was an able preacher, a concerned, loving pastor, and he endeared himself to the members. To those who had known his mother and me before we married, he was a son. To those who had grown up with him, he was a brother. He continued to work with SCLC and went to several cities on SCLC's behalf after they all returned from the Poor People's Campaign in Washington. He was implementing his plans at Ebenezer, and Ebenezer was responding to his leadership. Bunch and I were happy about what we were witnessing, because indeed we believed "that God never closes one door but what He doesn't open another."

For the first time, all of my grandchildren were in Atlanta. Their presence was a healing balm for me. We all felt that Coretta and her children needed us, and we gave her our love and support. It was hard without M.L., but we had to "keep keepin' on."

Then tragedy came to us again!

A.D. drowned in his swimming pool during the night hours of July 21, 1969. His oldest boy Al found him at dawn. It was Al's seventeenth birthday.

The morning he died, his son Al called my home, shouting into the phone that there was so much trouble at his house, trouble, trouble, he kept repeating. I dressed quickly and drove over there. Bunch could not go with me. She had to wait. It was too much, at that point in the early morning when Al called us—too much for her to think about. It was an answer to a question she just could not bring herself to ask. So I left her sitting there at home, alone, silent. I reached A.D.'s home as a fire department unit was arriving. They did all they could do, but he'd been in the water for several hours by then. Alveda had been up late the night before, she said, talking with her father, and watching a television movie with him. He'd seemed unusually quiet, she said, and was not very interested in the film. But he had wanted to stay up, and Alveda left him sitting in an easy chair, staring at the TV, when she went off to bed.

Now he was gone, and for me, of course, there was the instant rush of memories, the laughter around the house of those two little boys chasing and teasing their older sister. And the arguments, the changes in both A.D. and myself that brought us closer together, and brought him into the movement his brother was leading, a ministry that gave America the chance to become free. And so I missed them both. Standing there in A.D.'s yard, as neighbors began to gather, wanting to know what had happened, it struck me suddenly that I had to carry this terrible message back to Bunch, this message of how much she and I would have to miss both the boys now. *Help me, Lord,* I heard myself ask, and I started walking back home. *I need just a little help, my Lord,* I said to Him, as I started off to hold Bunch and tell her what had happened.

I had questions then about A.D.'s death, and I still have them now. He was a good swimmer. Why did he drown? I don't know—I don't know that we will ever know what happened.

* * *

I spent many days after A.D.'s funeral thinking about what had brought all of these things down upon us. God had willed us great opportunity, I felt, not great tragedy. We needed to be stronger, for weak people cannot face the sort of future this nation has already created for itself. The will to be better is needed, not just the tools, the mechanics and the machinery. These were the times when I thought hate might find a way to enter my heart. But Bunch and I were now duty-bound to keep each other's spirits from falling down. We had to keep the rest of our very young but emotionally matured family intact. And I worked at this as a life. I found so much strength in Al, A.D.'s oldest boy, who had to assume much responsibility with his father now gone on. Coretta surrounded her children with love and guidance during a time when a lesser person's feelings might have torn her apart and plunged her into the depths of a despair she couldn't escape.

Again, Atlanta showed its heart, as did persons known and unknown to us from around the world. Our own faith in God, added to the outpouring of love and sympathy that was showered on us, sustained us.

I refused to be bitter, and I refused to question God. At A.D.'s funeral, I told the world that "I had lost much, but I thanked God for what I had left!"

I still had a son, of course, in Isaac, and he was an anchor for the family in these great storms, not only for Christine, but for each of the rest of us. God had sent him all those years earlier, knowing we would need a man of character in times of hardship and sorrow. But it would be several years before I felt some ease to the agonizing the family was experiencing.

Fifteen

Back in the country, I had been a traveling preacher going from town to town, from pulpit to pulpit. In each place I'd find out what kinds of things had been going on, so that whatever topic I picked for a sermon would bring something to build up the spirit of those who heard me. This was a natural style in rural ministry, though not the only one. Some preachers tried to scare folks half out of their minds, keep them under control through fear. But I always enjoyed seeing a happy gathering leave my sermons, and if there were tears in anyone's eyes, I always wanted them to be tears of joy. Oh, the rumor is that I was very stern in the pulpit at Ebenezer, especially when I got on folks about their contributions. I'd pin down a successful businessman who joined our church and just tell him that the spirit of Ebenezer embraced the notion that members of the congregation made every effort to do business with one another whenever this was possible. There were more than a few folks at Ebenezer who prospered as a direct result of this spirit of community. And so I expected people who prospered in this way to be generous in support of their church. Most of them were; a few had to be reminded now and then. We had a fine church. Lord, Ebenezer has been a wonderful place.

But after my seventieth birthday, I had to give some serious thought to retiring from active life as a minister. I was planning to do a few lectures a year, some guest preaching now and then, but mainly I wanted to spend most of my time quietly in Atlanta, close to my wife. I was tired a little more often now. The race wasn't over, of course, but I knew it had been run for a lot of years.

The lectures took me flying a lot. This was the major difference for me between preaching when I was a young man and preaching during this period later in life. I'd be at a college in California one evening, and having dinner with Bunch and Christine and Isaac and their children in Atlanta the following night. To travel that far when I was a boy in Stockbridge would have taken more than a week. But the audiences weren't all that different. The things I had to say didn't change so much. People needed comfort and assurance, this has always been true all over this country. I told them simply that I was glad to be a part of America, and especially a part of the work that would make this a better nation. That was good work, that was a fine job to have.

And the response was always exciting. Young men and women at the colleges, couples, children, older folks in churches, many of whom came through the terrible fires of the American Sixties, managed to survive, and wanted others to know that it had been worth doing. And I certainly agreed with them, and told them so. There was a lot to talk about as America began moving through the Seventies. My words were spiritual, not political. I told folks that I never believed in political action that did not come out of a set of ethics, a sense of fair play, a high regard for the humanity and the rights of all people. There were students in northern colleges, for instance, who expected me to harbor a lot of anger and a lot of hatred for white people. And I said to them, as quietly as I could, that this wasn't true and never would be. My mother saw to that.

All those years back in the country, my mother, who had never learned to read or write or hear about philosophies and governments, told me things that moved across all the history of this nation as great wisdom. She told me not to hate. And this was something that kept me living. I found that after a time I even lost the capacity I thought I'd once had for hating. All people were my brothers and my sisters. And the feeling this gave me around people was a feeling of great strength and great pleasure. I enjoyed seeing so many people, and sharing with them. It made me believe deeply in the notion that if people talk to one another long enough, they can solve any difficulty that ever existed on the planet. But it takes time, and it takes an effort.

My travels began to heal parts of me that had hurt. Life always continues.

And then, just when I was beginning to feel some wholeness again, on a summer morning, the last Sunday in June of 1974, my Bunch was killed. . . .

I was awake early that day, lying in bed at dawn trying to go over in my mind the speech I was scheduled to deliver up in New Jersey late that afternoon. But it wasn't any thoughts of that speaking engagement that had wakened me. Bunch had experienced some difficulty sleeping at night, and I knew that she was greatly concerned about my traveling so much. But retirement was something I'd never been able to understand, much less practice. Keeping active was my way of keeping fit. Knowing that I still had much to share with other people in my country and throughout the world was a way of sustaining the spirit through difficult moments and memories.

Bunch worried, though. She'd say, for instance, that the weather was so unpredictable up North that I needed to take a warmer top coat, maybe some overshoes. This was her way of telling me how much she agonized when I went away, how much she dreaded each journey I was taking, so afraid was she that I might not return. Of course, she didn't want me to know how these feeling affected her, so she just fussed about my being dressed properly, or remembering all the schedules, calling when I got there or when I was ready to leave; staying in touch.

She carried that burden that only mothers can know, the burden that comes with losing children of whatever age.

That her sons were grown when they passed and had lived extraordinary lives didn't minimize the feeling that they were still her babies when they were taken away.

On that Sunday morning, I dressed very quietly as Bunch slept, stopping now and then just to look at her, hoping that she'd had some rest and some ease from her worries. Across the years the aches that move through life had burdened her and she hadn't wavered. Oh, it was difficult. We had held each other through moments when life seemed to be tearing both of us to pieces. There had been victories we'd gloried in, seeing Atlanta and the South and the United States become better than they had been, more than they were, and strong enough, we thought, to move ahead into being what many of us for so long had dreamed they could be.

We tried not to measure the costs in personal terms, but of course they were always there with us: the bombs, the guns, the clubs, the dogs and the jail cells. All these things remained, no matter how diligently we worked to put them aside. But at least we could, Bunch and I, consider that tears were now being shed throughout the South over the *same* things. Griefs could no longer be separated by color. Americans were now facing one another in the effort to discover just who they were and what this country was and would be. These tears, then, hadn't been shed for nothing.

I took my suitcase and forgot the topcoat I promised Bunch I'd take along with me, and I drove alone over to church. Along the way I saw families and individuals moving quickly to their own places of worship, black and white folks, children on their way, grown-ups hurrying them through the streets of Atlanta, streets that seemed to be changing over and over, becoming newer and newer since those days when I first saw the city, while riding in my father's wagon with all my brothers and sisters, bringing vegetables into what I thought was the biggest market in the whole world. All things were so much smaller now. Buildings I recalled as huge were tiny today. And, as usual, so much of what I saw reminded me of times M.L. and I had been here, or A.D. and I had passed by there . . . I missed both of them so much.

At Ebenezer that morning, I parked the car and stood for

several minutes talking with men and women who'd been members of the church for years, long enough in a few instances to have grandchildren who were growing up at Ebenezer. These folks had struggled with us, experienced joy and unhappiness with us, as we made our church into the solid, special place all of them knew. I shook hands, trying to remember faces and match them with names, looking at six- and seven-year-old boys and girls who could only be, from those features, descended from folks who'd been there at the church for as long as I had been.

"Daddy King!" they'd shout to me, the little ones, "Daddy King!" And I knew again from the sound of all this how Ebenezer constantly saved me, pushed me forward into all my days.

I sat in my study glancing through some mail that had accumulated for nearly a week, but a restlessness came over me, and for several minutes I paced the floor, trying to organize all the thoughts and expressions in my talk for later in the day. I prayed silently for a while, giving thanks to God that my strength was holding up. The traveling I did at my age was too much for many men years younger. Yet I was able to do it, and I was grateful to Him for allowing so much energy to remain in these later hours, when so many folks were just content to sit and wait. . . .

Going downstairs, I moved through the hallways and past the rooms of the church basement, where Sunday school classes were now humming along, and I felt myself wondering again just how many of those bright faces, among all those young ones, held a mind active enough to lead America. Oh, there were some, I could sense it in the questions I heard them asking, in the very serious contemplation they gave to the stories in the Bible that would form the base of their religious conviction and their commitment to justice, to freedom.

Suddenly, though, I felt another presence, one I couldn't really identify clearly. Several minutes passed as I looked through the classes, one by one, and saw the faces of people I didn't know very well. But, I thought, Ebenezer is a church that attracts folks from everywhere, from other churches and from lives without the worship of God to sustain them. I'd always felt good inside when someone told me how much coming to Ebenezer had meant, how much of a search had been ended when he or she found our doors.

I was about to return to my study when the classes began emptying out. Soon after, the basement was filled with dozens of young people, some of them calling to me and being cautioned by the Sunday school teachers to behave. I tried to look at them sternly, but there was too much love for that, and they saw one tiny smile after another form on my face. So many of the little children of Ebenezer returned them to me with a little wave here and there to let me know they were with me. Then, something seemed to brush past me, a quick, cool wisp of air. A number of young men and women took the Sunday school classes. Many others that I didn't always get to meet personally before they started with us taught these classes. And now, from within that moving crowd that surrounded me, I felt someone watching me closely, someone I could not yet pick out, but someone I could feel was following every move I made.

My eyes came to rest on several strangers, unusually tense young men who weren't really to be called visitors. They smiled, too, but in ways that seemed to express no happiness, no hope, and no joy whatsoever. And as I moved toward a staircase to start back up to my study, there was a pair of eyes . . . turning away, being swallowed up in the crowd, but somehow, through all of that, watching me steadily. . . .

In my study again, I tried to put the feeling of tension out of mind and spirit. But it remained. I could hear the organ now, and I knew that Bunch had arrived and started to play. More than an hour had passed since I arrived, much more, and the time had been swallowed up by all these concerns, which I suddenly felt were foolish and unnecessary.

The organ sound blossomed and was filling Ebenezer as I entered the main sanctuary. The church pews were filled, a few latecomers were at the back peering through the rows for one final seat that had not been taken. I moved alongside the pulpit area, where my grandson Derek, who was now a theological student, was seated with our guest minister for that morning, the Reverend Calvin Morris. Christine was seated in the first pew to the left facing the pulpit, and as I started there to join her, something held me for a moment. I leaned against the piano near that side of the church and stared across the sanctuary toward the raised platform that holds the Ebenezer Hammond organ. (We were buying a new pipe organ, and it was still being built.) Bunch was playing, very quietly, and I stared at her, seeing my times and hers blended together in that moment and so many others. We were at the point in the service where the Lord's Prayer is chanted, and we had completed only a few measures of the chant. And then, that awful moment began. It started with a voice none of us had heard before that raised up and shrieked through the sound of the music.

"I'm taking over here this morning!"

Then, a popping sound, and Bunch cried out. I saw her hand fly up to her face. Blood came through her fingers. I saw the eyes again, those wide, angry eyes. They belonged to a young man I'd seen earlier, one of the strangers who had come to our church that morning, and who now was standing in a pew near Bunch, waving a pistol in the air.

Later I would realize that if he'd only stopped after that first shot, if he'd run away, things might have turned out differently.

Now I was standing. I started walking to that side of the church when more shots rang out, one of them whistling past the side of my head. But I was moving toward the stranger. I could see Bunch falling forward, now holding her side. Motion blurred in front of me, arms waved, bodies scrambled about as everyone sought cover. Now I couldn't see Bunch, there were so many people moving around me, hands grabbing my arms and pulling me.

"I can't leave here without Bunch!" I heard myself shout as several of the church deacons pulled me backward, away from the pulpit. Derek jumped down and was tackling this young man as I was yanked nearly off my feet, still crying out that I wouldn't leave my wife there, struggling to get over to where she'd fallen now, across the organ.

The police and ambulances were called. Mayor Jackson came to the church and comforted the congregation, which was in a state of shock at what they had witnessed.

Just a few minutes later I was in a police patrol car, speeding behind an ambulance carrying Bunch to Grady Memorial Hospital. We rushed through streets I'd seen all my life. Now they were blurred into a forest of stone and metal and glass I felt I'd never seen before. I could see nothing, not even sense anything, except Bunch and the years and all the love and hopes. I knew she was hurt badly and of course I prayed hard as we moved quickly through Atlanta toward the hospital. The red light of the ambulance seemed to be jabbing through the car window at me. Suddenly the ambulance slowed down, almost to a stop, and I realized the car I was in was parked at Grady. I ran to the ambulance as they were getting her out on a stretcher. There was a lot of blood; I knew without asking that her wounds were very bad ones. She tried to speak when she saw me, tried to tell me where it was hurting. But the words wouldn't come out, just a gasping sound from deep within her.

I sat alone in a small office on the ground floor of the hospital and waited. It seemed like months passed, but it was just minutes later when a young doctor came into the room and said, "I'm sorry, Reverend King, we just couldn't save her. All of us tried, but it was just too late."

Deacon Edward Boykin was also fatally wounded that morning, and three other members were wounded.

I faced some difficult days following Bunch's passing. My family saved me during this period. Both Christine and Coretta remained in constant touch with me, as did Naomi. They saw that I was so busy doing things with all the grandchildren that I never had time to feel down or upset. The presence of the young is a huge comfort during such times. I was fortunate— and I was grateful.

The solace, hope, and love that we received from people around the world at the time of Bunch's tragic death was a reservoir of strength and consolation to each of us in the family. Each family member had his or her set of friends who said, "Whatever you need, don't fail to let me know." Then there were the persons who were friends to all of us, collectively, and of course there were the Ebenezer members. In six brief years, the Ebenezer family had experienced more pain and sorrow with us than many congregations experience in a generation. I remembered, if our pains have been numerous, our joys have come in multitudes.

I thought about the beginning of my family. I was determined to be the father to my children and the husband to my wife that my own father had not been able to be. I remembered the discussions at meal times, the pride and thankfulness that Bunch had taken in the growth of the children. My mind went back to the trips we had made as a family—any parent knows that traveling with three children in a car is an unforgettable and patience-trying experience. I saw us worshipping together and supporting each other in our individual endeavors—the five of us had been so close. Now there was only Christine and me. Oh, yes, there were my son-in-law, my daughters-in-law, my grandchildren, and the other family members, but my family, the bond which I had forged, was again broken, and this time it was Bunch who had been taken away.

Christine had always been such a tower of strength. Before M.L. and Coretta married, Christine and Coretta developed a bond of friendship which would be deepened and strengthened over the years. She loved her brothers and was always present when they needed her—at their homes which were bombed in Alabama, at their installations in Montgomery, in Newnan, in Birmingham, in Louisville, and at Ebenezer, where she was as diligent and dependable a member as any pastor would want in his membership. Christine was her brothers' sister, but she was also their friend.

It was she who went to New York with Coretta when M.L. was stabbed, she marched with him, she was with him in Oslo, and she traveled with Coretta and the others bringing M.L. home from Memphis. She went with me when I was called to A.D.'s home after he drowned, and she witnessed her mother being shot. I was watching her receive the callers at our home—people from all ranks of life came. Mrs. Rosalynn Carter was among the first to reach us that Sunday afternoon. Friends from the childhood and college days of my wife, business friends, public officials, my ministerial colleagues, college presidents—there was no end to the continuing flow of those who felt our grief. Christine was the gracious hostess whose strength emanated to each person whose hand she shook. The mantle had fallen on her, and she who is committed to duty and responsibility and who always says, "You do what you have to do," was doing just that. She took the lead in arranging the programs for two services that were held for Bunch. The finalizing of each detail was hers, and she knew the persons to contact.

The pain was deep and piercing, but the exquisite beauty of the flowers, the eloquence of the spoken words, and the ethereal quality of the music—the music that was Bunch's life—brought indescribable solace to us on Tuesday evening at the memorial service in Sisters Chapel on Spelman's campus, and the next day, July 3, at Ebenezer.

Our confidant and spiritual leader, Dr. Mays, delivered the eulogy that evening, and we could not have asked for more comfort than he brought in his unmistakably wise and consoling statements on the meaning of life—Bunch's life.

On Wednesday, it was Sandy Ray, my best friend, my friend from college days, my friend who could not attend our wedding because he didn't have a suit he thought was good enough to wear, who gave the eulogy. As I sat and listened to Sandy, I thanked God that he let me so live that during what seemed like unbearable grief there was a Sandy Ray and countless others whose strong arms of love had been thrown around us to keep us from falling.

It was a beautiful service. The program was printed on pink paper because Bunch was music and pink is the color for music. The music and the musicians that Bunch had taught were never better. And, yes, there was even laughter at the funeral!

Bunch had a boundless sense of humor, and Dr. Melvin Watson, who had known both of us before we met, recalled that very recently Bunch had said to him, "Melvin, I don't understand what is happening to King. When he met me, he said he was five years *older* than I was. Apparently he has forgotten that, because for the past four or five years he has changed his age so much that he is now five years *younger* than I am! Do you think you can talk to him and help him get the years straight?"

I was proud of Christine; her faith shone as it had never shone before. She gave me more attention than I thought I deserved.

She had always talked to her mother and me each day—in fact, she often came to the house each day—but now she did not let a day pass without spending time with me. She saw to it that I stayed on my diet, kept my appointments with the doctor (sometimes she made the appointment for me when I rebelled against making it), gave instructions to the housekeeper which sometimes included calling her, Christine, if I decided to go out when I had been told to stay in. Christine has borne great sorrows with grace, and I thank God for a daughter who has loved and cared for me while making a life for herself and her husband and children.

It was time for me to retire from Ebenezer. My energies were not what they had been, and I did not want the church to decline under my leadership. Bunch and I had discussed retirement many times, and in 1972 she had formally relinquished her role with the Music Department.

At our annual church conference in November 1974, I recommended the Reverend Joseph Lawrence Roberts, Jr., to the membership. Joe was born and reared in the African Methodist Episcopal Church, where his father was a minister. Joe's mother was a public school teacher; he has one sister.

Joe was a graduate of Knoxville College in Knoxville, Tennessee, where under the influence of the Presbyterians, he was invited to join their denomination. He accepted their invitation and continued his education, earning degrees from Union Theological Seminary in New York City and Princeton Theological Seminary in Princeton, New Jersey. Johnson C. Smith University in Charlotte, North Carolina, awarded him an honorary degree.

My recommendation, if the church accepted it, would mean that Joe would have to join the Baptist church. The members accepted my recommendation, and after many hours of prayer and consultation, Joe agreed to the call, joined Ebenezer, and was baptized by me on Sunday, January 5, 1975.

This unprecedented act created considerable media interest on the local and national scenes. A new pastor at a church seldom receives more than a release in the local and church papers. But in the case of a new pastor at Ebenezer, the story appeared in *Time* magazine, several issues of the daily Atlanta papers, and the denominational organs.

I knew there would be criticism of this unusual position which we were taking by calling and baptizing Joe, but I couldn't let this stop me. I had to stand by what I felt was best for the church. We had endured too much, struggled too hard, and come too far for me to be constrained by denominational ties.

Joe was based in Atlanta as a director in the Presbyterian Church, U.S., and he was introduced to us by a mutual friend, the Reverend William H. Gray III, pastor of Bright Hope Baptist Church in Philadelphia. In addition to his pastorate, Reverend Gray now serves as the United States Representative from the Second District of Pennsylvania. Occasionally Joe would come to Ebenezer to preach for us because I found my schedule too heavy to preach each Sunday. For the first time since 1960, I had been without a co-pastor; my sons were gone, and the Reverend Otis Moss, Jr., whom we called in 1970, remained with us only a short while. So I was alone, and I needed assistance.

Very gradually, so gradually that we were hardly aware it was happening, Joe began to be a part of the Ebenezer family. Soon he was an *integral* part of the Ebenezer family. In fact, he and Bunch had developed such rapport that we asked him to officiate at her memorial service in Sisters Chapel at Spelman College. She had heartily approved him and knew of my plans to recommend him to the membership.

I was confident that Reverend Roberts was the pastor and preacher Ebenezer needed. He was coming to us as a wise and experienced pastor who the Presbyterians were releasing with great reluctance. He would bring to Ebenezer the breadth of vision which a church of Ebenezer's influence and fame would have to have if it were going to continue to grow. He would have no problems keeping his focus on the cross. The church had become such a tourist attraction that I had to be certain its mission was not lost. Finally, Joe had had broad administrative experiences which would be essential to the ongoing programs of the church.

In an impressive and meaningful installation service, the Reverend Joseph Lawrence Roberts, Sr., delivered the installation sermon when his son assumed the pastorate of Ebenezer on Sunday, September 14, 1975.

❉   ❉   ❉

In the fall of 1975, I was invited to address a joint session of the Alabama state legislature, the first Negro in history so designated. I traveled over to Montgomery with a few misgivings. It was such a different place from what it had been just twenty years earlier, when the bus boycott started. Still, it was difficult to forget that M.L.'s church, Dexter Avenue Baptist, where I would also be speaking later that day, was located within sight of the capitol, where all the machinery of resistance to our freedom struggles had been based.

I arrived for a press conference in the middle of the afternoon, and was met by several members of the legislature's Black Caucus. During the conference, held on the steps of the capitol, a reporter asked if I intended to meet with the governor, and I realized that in back of me in the huge white building in downtown Montgomery sat George Wallace. Well, a meeting was arranged, although none had been scheduled originally. I walked into his office with all the armed security guards present, and the enormous portraits and banners hung from the walls, the state seals, wood paneling, the huge desk that almost hid him from view at first.

Wallace's eyes, I suppose, were the key to his condition. There was a deep sadness there, and I felt I was standing near a man who had had driven home to him the cost of appeals to violence in a nation with so many guns. We chatted. He was an old country boy, and we both knew of the cold and the hunger and the fear in places where so many were ground under the heels of landowners. He seemed pleased to see me and quickly explained that he'd never been against the Negro, but only stood for the law in a time when the law, possibly, was unjust. He said he regretted many things, most especially that few had ever understood his opposition to the federal government's plans for integration, which he conceded he knew was inevitable. I listened, and then said to him that he would receive my prayers because he surely needed them, and many more. At this time he still entertained the hope of running for the presidency, to speak for the little man, the folks who didn't dislike Negroes but just didn't want to be pushed around by the bureaucrats in Washington.

It surprised me that he looked so robust, so vigorous, until the wheelchair in which he sat was visible. The man would never walk again, and perhaps his dream was to be another Franklin Roosevelt. But too many people remembered those times, a very few years ago, when George Wallace would not move from a doorway to let integration take place at the University of Alabama. Most would remember that, not that this university was now fully integrated.

Wallace had been wrong in a time when news traveled instantly to every part of the world. He was an early television politician, who used that medium to appeal to people's fears and to ignorance in some parts of society. When he tried to keep some young Negro students from entering the University of Alabama, television newscasts made George Wallace a familiar figure to people who might never have known who he was by reading about him in the papers. Television, of course, does that. It creates personalities, and shapes them, and sends them around the world. This is what it did for George Wallace, who stood for what everyone would soon repudiate, publicly at least, in a way that could never be fully erased from memory. And so he was a sad figure. If he had, indeed, seen some light in his lifetime, it had shone too late for his greater political ambition. He'd remember that, in all those days in that wheelchair—being on the side of pain instead of healing, then coming to know so intimately what a mistake he had to carry through the future.

Quietly, he asked that he remain in my prayers, this was most important to him, and of course I assured him I wouldn't forget.

My speech to the joint session was brief because I know how legislators hate to waste any time when there's work to do for their constituencies. Twenty years after the tears and the blood, I stood up to a standing ovation and told them God planned to smile on them as they accomplished, as they kept the faith, as they saw to it that nobody wasted any tax dollars.

And that night at Dexter Avenue Baptist Church, in my son's former pulpit, I offered the text of remarks I'd made often during those months. "Once," I said, "as a young preacher I worked hard at preaching to move people. Now I want to preach and have people think." And I went on to say, as I would so many times afterward, that it concerned me that people were about to become *too* black, when they knew very well that some people had hurt us because they were *too* white for too long. I continued, "You and I know these are bewildering times we live in. But don't you lose your way and don't you ever let it get so dark you cannot promote a song."

There are two men I am supposed to hate. One is a white man, the other is black, and both are serving time for having committed murder. James Earl Ray is a prisoner in Tennessee, charged with killing my son. Marcus Chenault was institutionalized as deranged after shooting my wife to death. I don't hate either one. There is no time for that, and no reason, either. Nothing that a man does takes him lower than when he allows himself to fall so far as to hate anyone. Hatred is not needed to stamp out evil, despite what some people have been taught. People can accomplish all things God wills in this world; hate cannot. If we achieved a victory in the South it was over inhumanity. When the evil heart of segregation could beat no more, it was because it had been stopped by people who did not counsel violence, who did not brutalize and bomb, who never sought to take away any part of anyone else's identity as a human being. These things triumphed over the exaggerated power of hatred. And so which path would any man who knew this choose to travel? Hatred did not win. I prefer to share triumph.

I am asked if I think of Ray and Chenault, and in what way. And I say that I have never believed that Ray was alone in his plan. In my heart I can only wonder why there seems to be so much that points to others working with him. Why? That question is always there, of course. But M.L. had done what he set out to do, and I love what my son taught me and thousands of other people in this country about the enormous personal power of nonviolence. I love the lesson too much to make room inside myself for the very emotion that killed M.L. And it is again heartening to realize that he, better than anyone else, could have understood this.

I retired from the active ministry in 1975, and a Sunday in my honor was held at Ebenezer on July 27 of that year. It was

a beautiful and very moving day, bringing back memories that filled me with deep and abiding emotions. I knew it was time for me to move on and make room in that pulpit. I didn't want to leave. But I was thankful that I wasn't a stubborn old mule of a country boy anymore, and knew just when it was time to step aside.

My joy over this wonderful Sunday was not to last long, however. Just a year afterward, in July of 1976, my granddaughter Esther Darlene, A.D. and Naomi's fourth child, suffered a heart attack while jogging with friends in Atlanta. She died before help arrived.

I was away on a speaking tour in Indiana at the time, and the news reached me and Darlene's brother Al, who was traveling with me. We grieved together while waiting nearly all night for a flight home. It was rough for Al; he lost his little sister, whom he'd always been very close to. I knew it was a terrible blow for him—it seemed so unfair. But it had been God's decision. We had all been through such times before. And we'd learned, Al especially, I think, that life gets harder and harder as we move along. You can only continue and be what you can best be, and never give up trying to be better, no matter how many times you are pushed down.

Through that night, waiting with my grandson for a plane back to Atlanta, the pain continued, but so did my determination not to fall apart.

Throughout the last weeks of 1975, I spent as much time as I could bringing Ebenezer's new pastor into his role at the church. The transition was a smooth one. Reverend Roberts, although trained in the Presbyterian faith, developed an immediate rapport with members of the Ebenezer family, so I was able, after just a few weeks with him on board, to spend most of my time with the correspondence we still received from around the world, and some of the smaller details of the church's operation.

We chose Reverend Roberts because he impressed us with his knowledge, his commitment, and an extensive theological background. Ebenezer's tradition was one that stressed a trained ministry. Reverend Roberts helped us continue this tradition.

One afternoon my secretary, Miss Lillian Watkins, buzzed my study to say that former Georgia Governor Jimmy Carter was on the telephone. I'd always had a pleasant relationship with him while he was in office, sort of one country boy to another, and I was pleased on this occasion to hear from him. We exchanged a few stories about our children and my grandchildren, the way men will, and then he asked if he might drop by later in the afternoon.

Carter arrived while I was in the middle of a short nap. Miss Watkins rang me, then brought him up to the study. We chatted very warmly for several minutes, and I sensed after a time that this was more than a social call. I'd visited him at the governor's mansion, found him a fine host and a stimulating conversationalist. I'd also learned that he didn't do a lot of visiting himself without a purpose.

"Reverend King," he finally said to me, "I need your help with something. I need some advice." He went on to say that his time in the governor's office had given him a good deal of confidence about his leadership ability. And he wanted to know if I'd support him if he decided to run.

"Run for what?" I asked him.

"Why, for the presidency," he answered.

"The presidency?" I said. "Of what?"

"The United States," he told me.

I had to admit to some surprise. A southerner in the White House was something not many folks thought much about. It hardly seemed like a solid possibility in the modern American political atmosphere. But as we were talking I recalled how impressed I'd often been with Lyndon Johnson, a southerner if there ever was one, but a man who'd looked further than the convenience segregation had often provided him, and sought, vigorously and, I always felt, sincerely, to bring a new atmosphere and new solutions to some of this country's more serious social problems. His war on poverty had not been a glowing success, but in my view much of the failure he experienced with it had to do with general resistance and very poor management of many of the programs. Until that time, few people in this country had been involved with delivering real services to the poor and the disadvantaged of America. But Johnson could recall a childhood spent in the dust of Texas, growing up without enough to eat or wear during his early years. He knew. He understood firsthand what many others only dealt with at second-hand.

Now, seated with me in my office, was a smiling, friendly Jimmy Carter, asking for my help. How far it seemed from Stockbridge at that moment when he said that he felt if I supported his candidacy, he could begin a campaign of very real substance throughout the South and beyond it. He felt he could win. I remembered that he had been in the legislature years earlier, and had never been characterized as a "cracker" lawmaker, the way so many rural statesmen had been. And later, as governor, he achieved an unusual reputation among blacks. They talked about his availability while in office; they talked about his willingness to meet with people and work long hours on issues and needs as they were expressed by Negroes from around the state. But President of the United States? I hesitated, wondering if my old friend Nelson Rockefeller was really planning to make a run for the Republican nomination. I was in the Democratic party, but I'd certainly have no hesitation about crossing party lines for someone I thought could handle the kinds of political climate that black people were going to continue creating through the coming years.

There were two points, of course: Could he get the job in the first place? And could he perform well if he did?

"Governor," I said to Carter, "I'll tell you what. I'm pleased that you've come to me, but I have to be honest with you and say that only if a certain Republican does *not* run could I consider lending my support to your candidacy. Otherwise I'd have no problem with it at all."

I traveled to New York City for the Democratic Convention during the summer of 1976. My full commitment to Carter's candidacy was official by then. I had campaigned somewhat for him and was asked to deliver the benediction for the closing of the convention in New York's huge Madison Square Garden. I wasn't doing Jimmy Carter a favor by going there. He was the best man running for the office, and I wanted to see him elected. To me he was not only a symbol of how much the South had changed in my lifetime, but also a man who understood and accepted great challenges in an effort to shape the country's future. Who in this world believed he had a chance when he started out? And how many people thought, when I was a boy, that segregation would be gone before my life was over?

Carter and I could be split apart on certain political issues, and I knew we probably would be. But in my heart I felt certain he was the right man for the job he was after. In the weeks leading up to the convention, I spoke in several cities around America, urging folks in Negro churches especially to get behind Carter's presidential drive. There was very little resistance to my support of the man. Negroes knew the difference between white southerners like George Wallace—whom I never, never would have endorsed for the presidency—and Jimmy Carter, who in a few minutes' conversation showed that he was made right and had a lot of truth and decency in him.

I don't really know how much my endorsement influenced the outcome of that election. Carter won. And black voters turned out in considerable numbers for the Carter-Mondale ticket. The cynics, of course, said almost anything was possible after the disillusionment the country went through as a result of the Nixon Administration, and the Ford presidency it left behind. Carter, though, is a really good man, I've always thought. There can be disagreement with a good man, and certainly this is true with him. But only a good man can keep your respect while you are disagreeing with him. I feel that way about Carter. He wants a country living in harmony, spiritually intact, healthy and energetic. A lot of people in public life say they want these things. Disagreement arises over how we should achieve them.

Now the very core of American democracy is participation by all citizens in the processes of government. No one person has complete control at any time, and the President of the United States is no exception. To get anything done, of course, requires influencing rather than overpowering folks. And that is a very slow-moving activity. I am reminded often of that elderly eye doctor who gave me those glasses when I was studying at Bryant so many years ago. He wanted to be right; he wanted to be fair. But it was hard to do this when others were watching, because so many of them were afraid to believe in justice. And when everything political has been said about Jimmy Carter, I don't believe anyone will say of him that he was afraid.

I was pleased that Jimmy Carter won the election. And early on the morning of his inauguration I delivered some brief words, speaking in front of the Washington Monument. I felt honored and proud to play a part, however small, in such a great event.

My great respect and admiration for the Kennedy family notwithstanding, I support Carter's reelection campaign in 1980 one hundred percent. Coretta traveled with me to Washington during the fall of 1979, and we visited Ted Kennedy's office in the Senate. I considered it a necessary courtesy under the circumstances. Every person who aspires to the Oval Office has to seek support among Negroes. And I think most candidates realize that Negroes in America are still going to be found in great numbers within church memberships across the nation. Those churches are in touch with one another, even beyond denominational lines, on matters of national and international interest to American Negroes. It's very simple arithmetic, really, the kind I used to struggle mightily with back at the Bryant School in the 1920s. But when you put flesh on numbers, they really do come to life and mean a lot.

Negroes are many millions strong in this nation. And as long as we are identified apart from other members of this society, it will remain vitally important for us to be vigilant and strong. The struggle does not end. We say we want it to end, but it doesn't go away, despite what we insist are our best efforts. America just hasn't tried as hard as she'd like to think. Getting rid of discrimination is not *that* hard. Americans have to look into their own souls and find out whether they've been doing righteous work or just some more wasting of time. Everyone knows *that* answer. Some will not say it and many cannot. But all of us know. And God certainly knows, right along with every living heart on this earth. With Him, there cannot be any white lies or any other kind. He can see right on through. And there are still folks in this country who imagine they are getting away with fooling the Almighty. There is talk of peace and whispers of war. He hears all of it. We hear only part. So, who's being fooled?

A dozen years after his death, M.L.'s work is not nearly done. In fact, it seemed more often than not the country was slipping backward, becoming separate all over again. Atlanta's high schools are all but segregated, just the way they had been as we entered the 1960s, a full *six years* after the Supreme Court decision in *Brown* v. *the Board of Education.* And that "season of suffering" M.L. described returns to us more and more, it seems.

The young Kings, I'm proud to say, are carrying on many of the traditions established by their elders. A.D.'s daughter Alveda has been elected to the Georgia state legislature and plans a life in politics. Derek, her younger brother, has finished his ministerial studies and will have a pastorate soon. Marty III, M.L.'s boy, is still pondering a church career, while working in Atlanta. His sister Yolanda is in New York, beginning an effort to become an actress. The other grandchildren are in school, though Al has dropped out of college to work. I love them all so much, just as I do my three great-grandchildren, Alveda's youngsters, Jarrett Ellis, Eddie Beal III, and Darlene Ruth Celeste Beal.

The King family remains close. We are going on ahead too. We all love life so much and glory in it as we glory in our God.

I am asked why I continue to believe in nonviolence, and I answer that it remains not one of the ways but the only way to victory over the forces of evil in this country. If we live for a sense of oneness, we will not have time for the violence of revenge or oppression. We have outlived war as man once knew it; Vietnam should have shown us that. We are left, whether anyone likes it or not, to work for world peace as the only insurance of our survival through this century.

And whoever carries this word must make the word flesh by living out the terms of sermons and prayers so that people can see love as an *action.* For so many older people, it is already—and this is extremely unfortunate—too late. Young people will have to create a world citizen, unrestricted by color, who can hope realistically for a better day. As long as an idea lives, we are all still alive. For myself, I continue to look toward a day when we shall have one world and one people, when far will not be far and long will not be long, when we live together, neither black nor white, but one. . . .

Index